OPPORTUNITIES FOR ENGLISH IN THE PRIMARY SCHOOL

Michael Lockwood

Trentham Books

First published in 1996 by Trentham Books Limited

Trentham Books Limited
Westview House
734 London Road
Oakhill
Stoke-on-Trent
Staffordshire
England ST4 5NP

British Cataloguing in Publication Data
A catalogue record for this book is available from the British Library
ISBN: 1 85856 046 2

Designed and typeset by Trentham Print Design Ltd., Chester and
printed in Great Britain by BPC Wheatons Ltd., Exeter.

Learner Services

Please return on or before the last date stamped below

CITY COLLEGE
NORWICH

2 4 MAR 2009

2 1 APR 2009

1 2 OCT 2009

0 3 MAR 2011

2 9 MAR 2011

1 5 MAY 2012

2 9 MAY 2012

A FINE WILL BE CHARGED FOR OVERDUE ITEMS

215 980

For Kate, Amy and Grace

Acknowledgements

I would like to thank Bridie Raban for originally suggesting some time ago that I should write this book (before a series of proposed changes to National Curriculum English complicated the task!). A big debt is also owed to Cliff Moon for his reading of drafts of chapters 1,2 and 3, and for the many helpful suggestions of his which I have incorporated. I am aware of having taken the idea for 'pen portraits' of classroom practice from Cliff and Bridie's *A Question of Reading*. Catriona Nicholson also read and commented on the Introduction and Colin Wells, at very short notice, did the same for chapter 5. I am conscious of a debt to many colleagues in schools and to tutors and students at Reading University for ideas developed there. I would like to mention in particular John Earish of Frideswide Middle School, Oxford, the creator of the Survival Day project mentioned in chapter 1 and other practical activities referred to.

Without the secretarial support of Pat Parry this book would still exist in draft form. Pat's interest in my writing and her assistance in word processing it over a long period went way beyond the call of duty. Thanks are also due to Roma Scrivener and to my wife Kate for typing parts of the book. Kate also contributed ideas and suggestions.

I also want to thank Kate, Amy and Grace for putting up with my frequent absences in body and in spirit which the writing of this book entailed.

Acknowledgement is also made to the following authors and publishers for permission to reproduce material from their work: Lorna Cunningham for the shape poem in Chapter 3; Cliff Moon and the Reading and Language Information Centre for the simplified miscue table in Chapter 2; the Centre for Language in Primary Education, Webber Row, London SE1 3QW for the grid reproduced in Chapter 1; Judith Crosher and Hodder and Stoughton for the extract from *Schools;* Brian Patten and Penguin Books for 'What Am I?' from *Gargling With Jelly;* Michael Rosen and Penguin Books for 'Rodge said' from *You Tell Me;* and Maureen Lewis, David Wray and the EXEL Project for the materials reproduced in Chapters 2 and 3. Crown copyright is reproduced with the permission of the Controller of HMSO.

Contents

INTRODUCTION

What is English?

English is unique in a number of ways. It is the only area of the curriculum which is treated as a subject in its own right yet is also the medium for teaching and learning in all other subjects. English is also peculiar in being a subject without any content. Unlike Maths or Science, the other core subjects of the National Curriculum (NC), English has no agreed body of knowledge which has to be taught in a certain order. English is usually said to have a spiral structure where children return repeatedly to the same areas of learning (giving a talk, reading a poem, writing a story) but at different levels of achievement throughout their school careers.

Although English is treated as a subject discipline under the NC there have always been those who questioned that concept. In primary education particularly, teachers have tended over the past 30 years to refer to 'language' or 'language development'. This broader description suggests an area of learning which goes beyond the discrete 'English lesson', spreading across the whole curriculum. It suggests a concern with the totality of a child's language use rather than with particular facets of it. It also implies that the language to be developed need not always be English.

Why teach English?

It is probably not surprising that the need to teach English at all has been questioned in the past and that as a distinct area of study it is a comparatively recent addition to the curriculum.

The Report of the Working Group, chaired by Brian Cox, which produced the 1989 NC for English, gives five different views of the purpose of teaching English:

- A *personal growth view* has at its centre the individual child and in particular the spiritual and emotional self of each child. The purpose of English teaching is seen as facilitating the growth of the personality through a developing experience of literature and language

- A *cross-curricular view* has the curriculum of the whole school at the centre. The importance of language in *all* subject disciplines is stressed and the responsibility of *all* teachers to support and develop children's use of language. The purpose of English teaching is to enable every child to have access to learning in every area of the curriculum

- An *adult-needs view* places the language demands of adult society at the centre and in particular those of the world of work. The purpose of teaching English is to prepare children for day to day communication and employment in an age of rapid technological change

- A *cultural heritage view* sees as central the works of literature which have traditionally been valued in our culture. The purpose of teaching English is to introduce children to this canon and to the moral, spiritual and aesthetic values it contains

- A *cultural analysis view* considers the processes by which meanings and values are actually conveyed in all kinds of texts, classic and popular, both literary and in film, radio and television. The purpose of English teaching is to enable children to understand the culture and society they live in.

The Cox Report stresses that these five views are not to be seen as 'sharply distinguishable, and... certainly not mutually exclusive' (p.12). They can be seen as points along a continuum with children's individual development at one pole and their social development at the other:

INDIVIDUAL DEVELOPMENT   SOCIAL DEVELOPMENT

personal growth view	cultural analysis view	cross-curricular view	cultural heritage view	adult-needs view

How should English be taught?

As well as being a useful way to examine one's preconceptions as a teacher of English, this continuum of views is a helpful framework for viewing recent developments in English teaching.

Brian Cox first became well known as an opponent of what he saw as 'fashionable ideas about teaching English' prevalent in the 1950s and 60s. He saw as damaging, ideas which claimed 'that children would learn to read naturally without the help of formal instruction, or that their writing should be the product not of craft but of free expression' (Cox, 1991 p.13) and lamented 'the decline in the teaching grammar' (p.153). He published these and similar views in the 'Black Paper' *Fight for Education* (1969).

These excesses of English teachers in and around the 1960s have become part of teaching folklore, elaborated with each retelling. Anecdotes abound about teachers setting fire to wastepaper baskets, faking accidents and provoking arguments to spark off their pupils' 'creativity'. However little fact may be behind these stories, approaches to English advocated in the late 1950s and 1960s certainly gave more explicit emphasis to the individual development end of the teaching spectrum and deliberately sought to break away from the traditional teaching of English through formal exercises in grammar, composition and comprehension of the pre-war years.

John Dixon's book *Growth through English* (1967) has become representative of its time in focusing on the 'creative potentialities of *all* children'. Dixon advocated the decline in grammar teaching which Cox regretted, seeing it as a false imposition on children's use of language. The growth model also introduced a variety of texts, literary and non-literary, into pupils' experience and promoted collaborative oral work in the classroom.

Under this 'personal growth' view, English first began to evolve into language development, in the primary school in particular. In the mid-1970s *A Language for Life*, the influential report of an enquiry led by Alan Bullock, extended the emphasis on the child's own use and experience of language to include a 'cross-curricular' dimension. Consideration of 'language across the curriculum' meant promoting a more interactive style of classroom communication which gave room for the language children brought with them. The work of James Britton, Douglas Barnes and Harold Rosen at this time demonstrated how teachers in all curriculum areas needed to build bridges between children's own language experiences and the linguistic demands of their school subjects.

Brian Cox's anti-progressive views expressed in the Black Papers may have been a factor in his appointment as chief architect of the English NC by the Conservative government of the late 1980s. However, by this time, Cox felt that the 'excesses' he had campaigned against had been 'banished from the best classrooms' by a 'sensible balance... between the formal and the informal' (Cox, 1991 p.13).

The Cox NC tried therefore to establish a broad church in English teaching, based on 'good practice' in the 'best classrooms', which could accomodate *all* the five views of English previously mentioned. Cox hoped that this 'broad approach' would promote a consensus and 'unite the profession' (p.21). The NC was seen as 'a starting point... not a strait-jacket' (p.18), enabling not restricting teachers, who would in practice be able to give different weightings to the different views in their classroom work. Evaluation of the implementation of the Cox NC over the years 1991-3 concluded that: 'There was general agreement that primary teachers were happy with the content of the Order'(NCC, 1993a p.5).

Opponents of the Cox NC, however, saw the balance it claimed to have achieved as actually a bias towards the individual development end of the scale. *The Case for Revising the English Order*, published by the National Curriculum Council in 1992, reaffirms the central position of English but reveals a different view of what it is:

> English is the most important of the NC subjects. The knowledge and skills involved in speaking, listening, reading and writing are critical to success in the education system and in later life (p.vii).

Here English is clearly being treated as a subject with definable knowledge and skills, and the rationale for its place in the curriculum is also clear: success in education and in adult life. As a statement of position this straddles the three views of English closest to social development, with correspondingly less emphasis on personal growth and cultural analysis. The revisions which were then proposed in April and September 1993 (DfE, 1993a and NCC, 1993b) put greater stress on knowledge of grammar and 'great' literature and skills in initial reading, spelling and handwriting and speaking Standard English. Areas such as Media Education, Drama and wider Knowledge About Language were no longer included as part of English.

The 1993 revisions were never adopted, to the relief of many English teachers, since the review of the entire NC overseen by Ron Dearing overtook them. Draft proposals for revising English as part of this overall 'slimming down' exercise appeared (SCAA1994a) which represented a slight readjustment of the balance, away from the heavy weighting given to cultural heritage and adult-needs views. The new NC which was published in January 1995 (DfE, 1995) represents a further partial widening of the curriculum again to readmit some of the excluded areas, strengthening references to media and drama, for example, and reinstating Knowledge About Language in part as 'Language Study'. The emphasis on Standard English, grammar and phonic skills remains, but their prominence is now more of a presentational one (being placed consistently first in lists of items given equal status in the document), and the need for overall balance and integration is stressed above all.

Teaching English in the Primary School

So far we've considered the place of English in the curriculum generally, without a particular focus on primary education. How, then, is English approached in practice at Key Stages (KS) 1 and 2 , those stages where language and literacy development assumes the greatest importance? If we look into the primary classroom we can see a number of different approaches at work 'on the ground', which can be matched up, to some extent, to the views of English teaching discussed:

> i)*English through topic work*: A mixed ability class of Year 5/6 children is following a topic on local history. The children are involved in field work, visiting nearby sites and buildings; they are researching the local environment using books, maps and computer databases containing census returns; they are preparing and conducting interviews with local people; writing letters and making phone calls; and will eventually present their findings in a series of class books to be displayed in a local library and in a school assembly.

> The children are using and extending their skills and experiences in speaking, listening , reading and writing to pursue their local history. However there is no English lesson as such going on. English is being used here to help deliver the aims and objectives of the chosen topic. This is an approach common before the NC where teachers would often try to integrate as many discrete subjects as possible into an all-embracing topic. The advent of a subject-based curriculum has not led to the demise of primary topic work, in practice. Now a more limited cycle of topics based on combinations of Science, History, Geography and other subjects tends to be repeated and English activities are often integrated into them, as in the local history and geography unit above. A resourceful teacher might also plan for fiction and poetry writing, for example, and class or group reading might be connected to the local topic (reading Jan Mark's *Under the Autumn Garden* (1977) or Gene Kemp's *Jason Bodger and the Priory Ghost* (1985), for instance.)

> English specialists are sometimes uneasy about this assimilation of their 'subject' to serve the needs of others. They fear the loss of

exclusively English time as English becomes a 'service subject' in this way under the pressures of an overloaded curriculum. Defenders of the topic approach, say it generates real contexts for language and literacy development.

ii) *English through skills practice*: A Y4 class is having an English lesson, timetabled for the same slot each week and referred to (slightly confusingly) as 'language work'. The pupils are working from photocopied sheets taken from a commercial English scheme. The children are in groups, each group working on sheets taken from different stages of the scheme. They are working individually, writing their answers into 'language books' to be marked later by their teacher. At other times in the week the class uses the same exercise books for comprehension practice, when they use individual cards from a box in the corner of the classroom. On each card is a short passage and questions to be answered after reading it. They also have a separate 'spelling book' where lists of words are kept to be learnt for a spelling test which the whole class has each week.

Here there is a distinctive English content to the lessons, which follow each other in a step by step progression. Skills-based teaching such as this can exude a satisfying air of orderliness: development through repetitive practice appears to be readily visible as movement through the various stages of a structured scheme, even if this may be extremely slow for some pupils. Opponents see this approach as an inefficient way of developing language skills, which, in addition to the demotivating boredom it breeds, ignores the non-linear pattern of children's progress. They point to the often observed phenomenon whereby skills correctly used in decontextualised exercises are not then transferred to children's own writing. The scheme itself, they would argue, is what is learnt rather than the skills it is promoting.

Although primary children may seem a long way removed from the adult needs of later life, the skills practice approach is attempting to meet those imagined needs of society by ensuring 'mastery of the fundamental skills of English language which are vital... for our economic growth and competitiveness' (DFE, 1993a p.71). The approach has been a resilient one in primary classrooms despite changing views of English teaching over the past 40 or 50 years. For many teachers it is a kind of 'insurance policy', a reinforcement of skills children are using in more stimulating literacy experiences, and again not often used to the exclusion of all other approaches.

iii) *English through literature*: A group of Y2 children is listening to their teacher reading from *The Jolly Postman* (1986) by Janet and Allan Ahlberg. The book contains letters addressed to fairy tale characters which the jolly postman is delivering and there is a linking narrative told in verse. The letters can be pulled out of their envelopes and as the teacher reads, she opens them and asks children to read them out.

The children have already started to search for the fairy tales which the book alludes to. They have been telling the stories from memory and reading out printed versions for comparison. They will go on to act out in small groups the meetings between the postman and the fairy story characters, showing how they react to the letters they get (a solicitor's letter for B.B. Wolf and a piece of junk mail from a supplier of goods to witches).The children will also collaborate in twos and threes to write other letters to fairy tale characters — a letter of apology from Goldilocks to the three bears, a letter from a building firm to the three pigs — which will be posted in a special box for collection by the jolly postman during the school's book week.

From the shared reading and response to a rich central text such as this, a plethora of speaking and listening, reading and writing activities are set in motion in the classroom. Not only that, but other curriculum subjects may be brought in too: Design and Technology and Science investigations into, say, making working models of the postman's bicycle or the construction of envelopes.

Primary teachers have been basing their language work on books for a long time. The expansion of the curriculum since the introduction of the NC foundation subjects has led to many teachers developing this approach, which is in line with the 'interactive' reading development strategies promoted by the Cox Report. This has allowed them to place literature, and English, at the centre of their classroom work again. A careful balance is needed, though, to make a book like *The Jolly Postman* or *The Lighthouse Keeper's Lunch* (1977) and others by Ronda and David Armitage, a meaningful central focus and not simply a weak context for following NC programmes of study.

A literature-based English classroom puts greater importance on a 'personal growth' model of English. Books are valued as an indispensable agent in children's intellectual, emotional, moral and spiritual development and personal response to texts is encouraged. A holistic view of language use and experience is taken, not one which makes a division into discrete sub-skills. However, an approach to English through literature can also lay the foundation for 'cultural analysis' of texts. In terms of the classroom illustration used above, older children might begin to think about how and why fairy tales vary in different countries; why they are considered suitable for young children; how they have been made into animated films; the roles of boy and girl characters in them and so on.

Used in a different way, of course, literature-centred activities can reflect a 'cultural heritage' view of English teaching. Some primary schools have introduced 'literary appreciation' lessons into their timetables, for example, in response to the 1993 proposals to revise NC English which recommended increased emphasis on 'great literature' in the classroom, especially Shakespeare. Here the activities are likely to involve less expression of personal response through practical activities and more acquiring knowledge of 'classic' texts (or extracts from them) and practising the literary critical skills and terminology involved in 'appreciating' them.

Any orthodoxy, slavishly adhered to, is likely to be self-defeating. Most primary teachers would use all three of the broad approaches outlined above at some time and would be unwise to see them as 'mutually exclusive', as Cox warned.

The English Specialist in the Primary School

Historically the primary teacher has been a generalist, teaching *children,* not subjects, in a well known phrase. For economic as well as educational reasons this has remained the status quo since the advent of primary schools. Partly as a result of the 1975 Bullock Report, however, primary schools began to see the need for appointing 'consultant language teachers' or 'language co-ordinators' to have responsibility for language development throughout the school. Although Bullock thought 'all teachers in the primary school must carry equal responsibility for language', it was a 'mistaken belief that any teacher can cope with all the varied aspects of English without additional training or specialist advice' (p.210). Here was a recognition that there was a role for an English specialist in the primary school, that it was not something 'anyone could teach'; however the role was seen as an advisory not a teaching one.

In the middle and combined schools, created mostly in the 1970s, the situation has always been different because of the presence of 12 and 13 year olds. Here it has been accepted practice that Y7 and Y8 and sometimes the 9-11 year olds receive specialist English teaching and the English co-ordinator fulfils that teaching role, usually still with mixed ability classes.

Recent discussion papers on the organisation of the primary curriculum have begun to suggest an extension of this practice. *Curriculum Organisation and Classroom Practice in Primary Schools* (DES, 1992) recommended more flexible thinking about teaching roles, urging consideration of specialist and semi-specialist teachers ('one who teaches his/her subject, but who also has a generalist and/or consultancy role' [P.43]). The pressures of a subject-driven NC have undoubtedly added to this revaluation of the position of the subject specialist in the primary school and some schools have responded by reorganising the Y5 and Y6 curriculum along middle or secondary school lines.

Proposals for the reorganisation of initial teacher education announced recently also seek to introduce greater flexibility into primary teaching. *The Initial Training of Primary School Teachers* (DFE, 1993b) 'welcomes and wishes to encourage the use of specialist teaching in primary schools, particularly at KS2', since 'lessons from specialists offer pupils a high standard of subject teaching' (pp.6-7). Although the above draft circular suggests that 'the benefits of timetabled subject teaching at KS2 are increasingly recognised' (p.1), at present only a small number of schools have taken up the suggestion of increased use of specialist teaching, including English specialists, according to the follow-up report to *Curriculum Organisation and Classroom Practice*. It remains to be seen whether the generalist/consultant English teacher continues in that role or whether in the future only *some* primary teachers will be English teachers and some English teachers will be primary specialists. Increasingly school-based initial teacher education courses will ensure any such development has an immediate impact on student teachers too.

English in the National Curriculum

This book follows the NC in referring to English as a subject, whilst keeping in sight the problematic nature of this status at primary level. It also follows the structure of the NC by dividing English into three main components, Speaking and Listening, Reading and Writing, to each of which a chapter is devoted, though the interrelationships between them are stressed. The intention at all times is to show how these parts are integrated together in actual classroom practice. Two other shorter chapters give additional attention to aspects of NC English which I feel need further development in the primary curriculum: Standard English and Language Study and also Information Technology and Media Education.

It is important to remember however that the NC, particularly in the 'slimmed-down' version of 1995, is not the whole of English. Teachers of English have always recognised that whilst the NC prescribed what all teachers must cover in the programmes of study, it did not proscribe other possible activities and approaches. Under the slimmer curriculum proposed, it is even more the case that teachers will need to incorporate the fundamental skills, knowledge and understanding set out there into a wider perspective. I hope in the chapters which follow, to outline some opportunities for doing just that.

Further Reading

Beard,R. (1993) *Teaching Literacy: Balancing Perspectives.* London: Hodder and Stoughton.

Tann,S.(1991) *Developing Language in the Primary Classroom.* London: Cassell.

Wray, D. and Medwell, J. (1994) *Teaching Primary English: The State of the Art.* London: Routledge.

Chapter One

SPEAKING AND LISTENING

The Background

> Oral work is ... the foundation upon which proficiency in the writing of English must be based; more than that, it is a condition of the successful teaching of all that is worth being taught. (p.71)

This is the conclusion not of the most recent report on National Curriculum English but of the Newbolt Committee on the teaching of English — reporting in 1921. Realisation of the central importance of children's spoken language, especially in the primary school, within the most important area of the curriculum, English, is not new. What *is* new is the legal requirement that work in speaking and listening should form a significant part of English teaching for all children, which became the case with implementation of English in the National Curriculum from 1989, nearly seventy years after the Newbolt recommendations.

Between these dates there was a long struggle to establish 'oracy' in English classrooms. The coining of the term itself, by analogy with 'literacy' and later 'numeracy', was part of the campaign to give speaking and listening equal status with the two traditional Rs of English teaching.

The Bullock committee of inquiry (1975), like Newbolt, saw as 'a priority objective for all schools ... a commitment to the speech needs of their pupils and a serious study of the role of oral language in learning' (p.156). But until the setting up of a National Oracy Project (NOP, 1987-93) to study language for learning in this way and specifically to develop spoken language in schools, there was no significant effect on classroom practice in the majority of primary schools. The NOP sought to promote the value of oral work and to develop teachers' skills in this area in terms of planning, organising and assessing oracy. This developmental work had a strong influence on the 'good practice' which the Working Group incorporated into the 1989 English curriculum, where 'Speaking and Listening' is included as AT1, described as:

> The development of pupils' understanding of the spoken word and the capacity to express themselves effectively in a variety of speaking and listening activities, matching style and response to audience and purpose.(p.3)

'Speaking and Listening' is retained as AT1 in the revised National Curriculum English of 1995 but in response to the Secretary of State's request for more emphasis on listening skills and on pupils' use of standard English, the description of AT1 is modified thus:

> To develop effective speaking and listening pupils should be taught to:
>
> • use the vocabulary and grammar of standard English
>
> • formulate, clarify and express their ideas
>
> • adapt their speech to a widening range of circumstances and demands
>
> • listen, understand and respond appropriately to others (p.2)

Children's Oral Language

The position of oracy in English in the National Curriculum reflects a growing awareness of the importance of children's oral language itself in terms of personal, educational and social development, as well as its importance as the foundation for literacy learning. Research projects, such as the 1977-81 Bristol Study, 'Language at Home And at School' (see Wells, 1987), have revealed just how much language children have actually acquired, *before* they begin compulsory schooling. By the age of about four, most children will have developed competence in the main functions and forms of spoken language, including most of the grammatical structures which characterise it. They will have developed their speech from its origins in one and two word utterances at about 12-18 months, to a level of comparative sophistication where they can command a vocabulary of several thousand words by the time they first go to school. This spoken language will, of course, be the language or dialect of the child's home community, which in most cases will vary slightly from standard English usage.

The oral language children bring with them at the start of their schooling and what the primary school and the primary teacher do with this language are of the utmost importance in terms of achievement not just in English but in all areas of learning. The Bristol Study and other research into children's language acquisition and development has highlighted the importance of social interaction in the early development of spoken language. Children seem to acquire language not only because of an innate predisposition or receptivity, or through simple imitation of what they hear but also, crucially, because parents and other carers provide ready conversational partners for their utterances from the very earliest age. Parents and other adults share, support and extend children's first attempts at language, treating these noises as meaningful (even profound!) and engaging in a continuous series of interactions with them by means of which spoken language seems to be acquired.

When children begin compulsory education, they have to accommodate the oral language expertise they have built up in this way, at home and in the local community, to the demands of institutionalised learning. Having learnt to talk, they now have to talk to learn. This *should* mean adding to what they can already do in terms of speaking and listening through further interactions in the classroom. It will certainly mean learning to use language in different ways and for different purposes than at home. For example, children will need, as pupils, to understand the conventions of classroom discourse where the ratio of adults to children may be 1 to 25 or 35 instead of 1 to 1. They will need to add new registers of speech to their repertoire to cope with the less familiar, less supportive contexts of classroom and school talk. Where children fail to make the transition easily from the home to the school language environment, there are likely to be serious problems in learning.

For the teacher, this highlights the importance of building bridges between the language demands of the primary classroom and curriculum and each child's own language resources. This will mean being aware initially of each child's spoken language competencies, be they in standard English, dialect and/or a different mother tongue. It will then mean demonstrating a respect for and appreciation of what each child individually brings to school in terms of (widely differing) capabilities in spoken language. Finally it will mean building on this foundation through classroom interaction and dialogue to develop children's spoken language as *the* tool for learning.

Standard English

Standard English, which most linguists would define as 'conventional' or 'standardised' rather than strictly 'correct' English, is likely to be the language (or more accurately a special kind of dialect!) used by the primary teacher. Standard English is that variety used for almost all writing. Standard English in speech is more problematic to define. It developed from regional dialects (the East and Central Midlands of the fifteenth century — see Crystal, 1994) but is now characterised by the fact that, unlike other dialects, it is *not* identified with any particular region. It is the language of national and often of world communication. Most often it is defined in a rather circular way as the language of education and of educated people (Trudgill, 1975), and so as a 'social dialect'. However, standard English does change over time.

In using standard English consistently and in occasionally flouting it for special effect ('You ain't seen nothing yet!'), the primary teacher will be constantly demonstrating and reinforcing a model of the type of spoken English which is most widely used in more formal situations. She or he will *not* be modelling Received Pronunciation, that way of speaking standard English associated with the public schools, Oxbridge and elocution lessons and spoken now by only about 1% of the population (Hudson, 1992). Standard English can be spoken correctly in *any* accent. What many primary teachers will provide, though, given their geographical mobility as a professional group, is often a new, slightly unfamiliar accent for children to assimilate as listeners (though not to imitate as speakers). This can be a source of amusement or embarrassment — or it can be a teaching point and a way into what the National Curriculum calls Language Study, formerly Knowledge about Language, through speaking and listening (see Chapter Four).

The National Curriculum made access to standard English an entitlement for all pupils for the first time:

> Pupils should have increasing opportunities to develop proficiency in spoken Standard English, in appropriate contexts (PoS for AT1, 1990. para 10).

The entitlement was not only to be able to speak standard English, when appropriate, but to know what it was as a variety of language:

> Teaching about language through speaking and listening ... should focus on ... the forms and functions of spoken Standard English (para 9).

As the language of national and international communication, it was seen as a vital element in children's language development. It was seen as an *addition* to the spoken repertoire of pupils, making them 'bi-dialectal' in most cases, not as a means of replacing undesirable or 'incorrect' non-standard dialects (Cox Report, 1989). In this respect the 1989 English curriculum was in line with the report of the Newbolt committee back in 1921. Despite the advocacy of explicit 'speech training' for infants in the Newbolt report, the attitude to standard English and dialect was an enlightened one.

> We do not advocate the teaching of standard English on any grounds of social 'superiority', but because ... inability to speak standard

English is in practice a serious handicap in many ways ... We do not, however, suggest that the suppression of dialect should be aimed at, but that children who speak a dialect should, as often happens, become bi-lingual, speaking standard English too (para. 69).

In the revised 1995 English curriculum children's use of spoken standard English is given more prominence and defined in terms of certain features of vocabulary and grammar. However, it is still made clear that children's learning of standard English and use of it in the classroom should not devalue their home accent or dialect

In order to participate confidently in public, cultural and working life, pupils need to be able to speak, write and read standard English fluently and accurately. All pupils are therefore entitled to the full range of opportunities necessary to enable them to develop competence in standard English. The richness of dialects and other languages can make an important contribution to pupils' knowledge and understanding of standard English. Where appropriate, pupils should be encouraged to make use of their understanding and skills in other languages when learning English (p.2).

The 1995 requirements emphasise the importance of exercising flexibility and sensitivity in introducing pupils to standard English. There should be no suggestion of speech training here. The picture should still be one of a primary classroom where children's home language is not being discounted as 'sub-standard' but where their range of spoken English is being extended through planned teacher support and shaping.

In the case of bilingual or multilingual pupils, of whom there will be some in all primary schools and a significant number in many, the principle of respecting the language the child brings to school and of using it to bridge the learning of a second language is even more important, as the NC suggests above. Research shows that appropriate use of the mother tongue in the classroom (though many bilingual children and their parents are reluctant themselves for it to be used) does not hinder but enhances learning of ESL. In its Non-Statutory Guidance (NSG) on bilingual learners (NCC, 1990), the English NC recognises this and points out that:

In implementing the programmes of study, different languages and different varieties of English should be valued and used in the classroom (para. 2.10).

'The linguistic and cultural knowledge of Welsh-speaking pupils' is similarly recognised as valuable in their learning of English in the 1995 NC (p.2). Later on, in considering Language Study, it will become clearer how pupils with more than one dialect or language are a resource, not a problem, in the primary classroom.

Speaking and Listening in the Primary Classroom

Classroom climate

If successful speaking and listening activities are to take place in the primary classroom, the right climate needs to be created from the outset. This involves the children's attitude to oracy work. Without an atmosphere of respect for oracy as a way of learning and appreciation of the value of co-operative group work, effective speaking and listening cannot take place.

Many teachers establish clear ground rules from the beginning, before trying to develop oral skills in their classrooms. This need not mean dictating a list of dos and don'ts to the class and establishing a model of teacher-dominated discussion from the outset. The children themselves can be encouraged, with appropriate support, to come up with guidelines for talk, as did a class of Y2 children whose teacher was involved in the National Oracy Project. The children produced as a poster for display in their own and other classrooms this set of 'rules' for talking in groups:

Don't keep comments to yourself
Help each other discuss
Keep trying, support
Co-operate, stick together
Don't leave anyone out
Give information
Don't shout
etc (Norman, 1990 p. 15).

This kind of activity in itself can constitute an ideal introduction to speaking and listening in groups. Children will need to be reminded to keep their guidelines in mind as discussion work develops in the classroom, and a poster on the wall makes this easy to do. Children can refer to their own rules too when asked to reflect on their own achievements as speakers and as listeners after taking part in discussion-type activities.

Let's go on to look now at a classroom where an atmosphere of respect for all children's language has been created, where speaking and listening skills are valued in learning and where ground rules for discussion have been firmly established by consensus.

The Survival Topic

A class of Y6 children are working in groups of four. Tables have been moved around in the classroom by the children themselves to make this easier. The groups have been selected randomly by the teacher — drawn out of a hat whilst the children watched. The children are working on a survival topic. Each group has to imagine that they are the sole survivors of an air crash and that they must work together as a group to survive on an uninhabited island until they are rescued. The children are filling in a journal at the moment, individually, so the classroom is untypically quiet. In their journals they are reflecting on how they feel their group is operating and how they personally have worked as a group member. In other words, though taking part in a simulation exercise where they have to act within an imaginary situation, they are now out of role and writing as themselves. These reflective, personal logs will be completed at regular intervals after each session of work on the topic and later read by the teacher.

As part of this Survival project, each group has had the same number of tasks to organise, such as designing a shelter; making a simple compass; devising a method of signalling to attract rescue; and finding the best way to filter water. The topic, in other words, is a cross-curricular one, bringing together, within a real and purposeful context, skills and concepts from such discrete National Curriculum subjects as Science, Geography and Design and Technology. With appropriate teacher support, the children have to use their skills as speakers and listeners to organise and carry out the required group tasks. At the end of the project there will be a 'Survival Day' when the groups will try to put some of their plans into practice and the school grounds will be covered with make-shift shelters. An agreed assessment procedure will use a points system for marking the various tasks, to determine who does survive and who does not!

Planning and Organisation

The Survival project illustrates a number of features of successful practice in oral work. Not only do the children participate as speakers and listeners in a meaningful activity, they also have the opportunity to reflect on and evaluate their achievements either verbally or, as here, in writing. This encouragement of self-awareness and self-assessment is vital to developing children's oracy.

The project also demonstrates that effective speaking and listening work does not just happen in the primary classroom; it has to be planned for and organised. Nor does it just happen in English lessons. In fact, of the three components of the National Curriculum English, AT1 is the one which lends itself most easily to being developed across the curriculum. This cross-curricular topic with Y6 has been carefully designed to incorporate speaking and listening activities. The planning and organising of this sort of work involves asking and answering the following important questions: why? who? and how?

Why?

Since talk needs to be about something as well as with someone, pupils need to know the purpose of any oral activities. Why are they working as they are? What kind of outcome is envisaged? Will there be a verbal or written report, an audio or video tape, or no actual product as such? Who is the likely audience for any outcome: the teacher, other groups, other classes?

Teachers will, of course, need to have worked out the answers to these questions themselves beforehand. In the case of the Survival topic, the children's group talk had a clear purpose, a practical outcome and an audience of teachers and other groups on the culminating Survival Day.

Who?

Once the purpose of the activity is established, the children will need to know who they are working with. Will they be in pairs, in small groups (3-6), larger groups, or working as a whole class? Will the groupings be determined by the teacher or pupils? According to age, gender, ability, language, friendship or at random? Has the class worked in this way before or will the organisation need to be carefully explained, perhaps even displayed? In the Survival topic the groups of fours were selected at random by the teacher.

How?

The classroom will now need to be adapted to fit the purpose and the groupings decided on. What arrangement of resources and of classroom furniture will best enable the chosen groupings to function properly? For effective oral work children will need face-to-face contact with partners or group members. Can the classroom environment be modified in any way (e.g. by the use of carpeting, curtains, drapes) to improve acoustics or reduce incidental noise? For the Survival week tables were moved into clusters of four, access to limited amounts of practical materials was staggered and provision of carpeting throughout the classroom significantly helped to reduce noise.

Once these three main organisational questions have been dealt with, two others also suggest themselves: when? and what?

When?

For talk to be meaningful sufficient time has to be allowed for it; all groupings, however familiar, need time to warm up or possibly to cool down! However, the stimulus of a clear deadline is also necessary to focus minds on the task in hand. The pupils will need to know at the outset how much time is available and need to be reminded of the approach of deadlines. The Survival topic was carefully planned over several weeks with deadlines for particular tasks to be accomplished and the ultimate deadline of the Survival Day.

What?

Finally, pupils will need to know what kind of speaking and listening the teacher has in mind. Will it be an exploratory, free-ranging discussion ('exploring, developing and explaining ideas' as AT1 requires) ; will children be speaking in roles or as themselves; will there be a chair with the job of arriving at a group consensus; is it a formal debate? Guidance will need to make this clear from the start since children will interpret speaking and listening tasks differently in the light of their own previous experiences. In the Survival work the talk within the groups was free-ranging within the parameters of the tasks set. The children had to organise themselves as groups; some elected group leaders, others operated on a co-operative principle. They were not asked to role-play particular characters.

Other contexts for speaking and listening

The Survival topic was effective because it was able to answer clearly all the key questions of planning and organisation mentioned above. Other ways of answering them are, of course, equally possible where different contexts for oral work are created.

In the programmes of study for AT1 in the 1989 English curriculum, 'a range of situations, audiences and activities' is recommended for the development of oral skills. The particular skills to be developed are listed in the Cox Report:

- Clarity and precision in describing experience and expressing opinions, and sensitivity in articulating personal feelings

- Formulating — and making appropriate responses to — increasingly complex instructions and questions

- A capacity to organise or sequence information and response

- Adjusting language and delivery to suit audience and purpose, and being able — as an audience for others — to understand, respond to and reflect on correspondingly wider modes of address

- An ability to function collaboratively

- An ability to be explicit about how written and spoken language can support each other. (Cox, 1989 para 15.16))

The close interrelationship between speaking and listening generally and between these identifiable skills in particular is stressed. Discrete skills are usefully distinguished as above for purposes of planning, organisation and, later, assessment, but in the course of practical classroom activities they will always be developed together and as a whole, in an integrated programme, as the 1995 NC requires.

Three main contexts are suggested in both the 1989 and 1995 curricula for the development of these oral skills:

(i) Situations where children participate as speakers and listeners in group and whole class activities (e.g. role-playing, group discussion).

(ii) Situations where children listen attentively and respond to what they hear (e.g. stories, poems, radio programmes).

(iii) Situations where children communicate with the teacher, other pupils or the whole class (e.g. telling 'news', story telling).

Some of these contexts will emerge from recognisably English activities but most will involve either one or more other subject areas, as in the case of the Survival work above. That particular cross-subject topic involved children in the first type of classroom context for the most part, developing oral skills through participating in small group activities.

(i) Other examples of this kind of collaborative group work might be:

Planning Inquiry

Y6 children work in groups of six to consider plans for building a new road in the locality. Each group is asked to represent the views of a local interest grouping — farmers, villagers, local councillors, businessmen, commuters, etc. — and has to present its case for or against the proposed road at a 'public inquiry' involving the whole class. This will be video-taped and later watched by the children and also by a local planning officer who will comment on the strengths of the various cases put forward. The children will also be asked to reflect on how effectively they felt they argued their positions, as individuals and as groups.

Fair Testing

A Y5 class works in groups of four to devise a fair way of measuring the relative strengths of supermarket carrier bags. Once the group has arrived at a method, this is used to test a representative sample of plastic bags. The groups must then communicate their findings and methods both in a written report and in an oral presentation to the board of directors of a supermarket chain, made up of the rest of the class. A decision is finally made on the choice of strongest plastic carrier bag from the findings presented. There is then a whole class discussion on the merits of the different 'fair tests' devised.

Planning a Party

A class of Y2 children is asked to work in groups of five to plan a Christmas party for a Y1 class. They need to decide on appropriate food and entertainment for the numbers of children involved. They are given a budget to work within and must make decisions about what can be afforded out of this. The various plans will then be considered by the Y1 children who will vote on which of the proposed parties they prefer.

It will be clear from considering these activities that the main oral focus is on the skills of collaborative group work, but that, as suggested, other speaking and listening skills are of course being developed, for example, adjusting language and delivery to suit audience and purpose, and increasing competence in the use of standard English.

(ii) Examples where the main focus of oracy activities is on children listening attentively and responding — a kind of *active* listening — abound in the primary classroom. Often these kinds of activities are literature-based, involving children listening and responding to stories and poems either read by the teacher or a visitor or broadcast on television or radio.

Responding to Stories

Pupils in a Y3 class have been listening to a reading of *The Shrinking of Treehorn* by Florence Parry Heide (1975). The story is about a young boy who is ignored by his parents and teachers to such an extent that they don't notice that he is getting smaller each day. The children play out in pairs various situations from the book based on lack of communication between parents and children, and then talk about similar episodes from their own experience. Then they act out ways in which Treehorn might be able to get his parents and teachers to listen to him. This role-playing eventually leads to a whole class discussion of difficulties in communication and the feelings this gives rise to, particularly the frustration felt when people do not listen. Other related stories are read, such as:

Not Now, Bernard by David McKee (1980)
Angry Arthur by Satoshi Kitamura and Hiawyn Oram (1982)
Where the Wild Things Are by Maurice Sendak (1967)
I Was a Class 2 Werewolf by D.Pinkwater (1992)

Paper Folding

A Y4 class are working in pairs, and in this instance sitting back to back. Each child has made a simple shape by folding paper. They are taking it in turns to give instructions for how to make the shape to the partner they cannot see using spoken words only (no gestures, pointing or use of diagrams) and receiving no feedback. Each partner is also, in turn, listening attentively and responding to the verbal directions given. At the end of the exercise the shapes are compared and the success of the act of communication is apparent. Whole class discussion follows about the skills of listening actively, as well as of explaining clearly, in a non-reciprocal situation.

Interviewing

A group of mixed Y5 and Y6 children are interviewing elderly members of the local community about their perception of social and cultural changes in daily life as part of a study of Britain since 1930. They have formulated careful questions as a group, with the help of of their teacher, and have discussed helpful strategies to use when interviewing members of the public. They are now each listening and responding as their elderly guests answer the prepared questions. The interviews are all taped and later the group will listen to them again and decide which information to extract. Careful transcripts will then be made of short extracts which illustrate important points about changes in the British way of life. These will later form part of an assembly presentation to the whole school and a hall display.

(iii) Again contexts for oracy which involve children communicating either individually or as a group member are numerous from the beginnings of primary schooling. The performative aspects of speaking and listening are often the main skills which are being emphasised in these sorts of activities, which may involve drama or recitation of some kind. Also common are activities which involve the presentation of information to an audience, such as the traditional infant 'news' sessions or junior 'show and tell' time. Other examples are:

Storytelling

Y3/4 children have listened and responded to oral stories from different countries told by the teacher and by a visiting storyteller. They have talked as a whole class about stories which are passed on by word of mouth rather than being written down, and how a story can be told effectively so as to hold the listener's attention. They are now telling each other familiar stories in pairs, either traditional tales they know by heart, 'true stories' from their own experience or stories they have made up. Later they will choose a story to tell to a small group of infants, and will prepare it by making notes and perhaps simple cue cards or pictures to help them in their performance. The juniors will re-tell their tales individually but work with the infant groups in the supportive context of their original pairings. (See NSG, 1990 section C5, for a more detailed example of a storytelling project.)

Lego Machines

Y1 children have constructed fantasy machines in small groups using Lego or Duplo kits. Once the constructions are finished, the groups will take it in turn to describe to the rest of the class, with appropriate teacher support, how their model machines work and what they do. The models will then be displayed in the classroom and used as the basis for early literacy work (the children dictating to the teacher or helper and then reading a sentence about the models).

Poetry Performance

As part of a Poetry Week, the whole school is involved in workshop activities led by teachers or visiting students, parents and writers. The children have watched a 'Poetry Show' put on by students from a local

University Department which has involved them acting out as well as reading out poetry texts. Next, in small groups, the children have been given copies of suitable poems for performance and, working with the students, have talked about ways of 'realising' the text and bringing it to life for an audience. The morning's workshop will end with each group of children giving a short performance of their poem to an audience of other children in the school. A member of staff is taking still photographs and making sound recordings as a record of the Poetry Week.

The contexts suggested here for developing oracy are ones which connect variously with the programmes of study of the core National Curriculum subjects Maths and Science and of foundation subjects such as Design and Technology, Geography and History. The PoS for these subjects often contain references to children using talking and listening for learning and to collaborative group work. The 1989 English PoS actually required primary teachers to:

> draw on requirements from across the curriculum, and in particular those existing requirements for mathematics and science which refer to use of spoken language and vocabulary, asking questions, working in groups, explaining and presenting ideas, giving and understanding instructions (p.23).

'Speaking and listening' itself, as a topic, can also be a fascinating and rewarding area of study investigated within the context of 'Sound' in Science, as suggested in the 1989 NSG for English (para. 4.11) or as part of Language Study.

Organising Groups

The classroom contexts suggested above give possible answers to the 'why?' organisational question, illustrating how oracy can arise in planned, meaningful situations across the primary curriculum. They provide a range of situations, activities and audiences, from peers to younger children to elderly people, as required in the English NC.

Those PoS also require the use of 'groups of different sizes' for speaking and listening work. The question of 'who?', over and above actual group numbers, also has a number of other possible answers. Many imaginative ways for grouping children have been devised by teachers working within the National Oracy Project (see NOP, 1991). It is probably wise not to over-elaborate with organisation of groups to begin with but, as teacher and pupil experience is built up, the following strategies could be used progressively to develop group oracy work:

Snowballing

Children begin a discussion activity in pairs, with a regular 'talk partner'. After a period of time this pair joins another to form a four; in turn (if appropriate) this group becomes a larger group of eight and so on until the teacher decides it is time to share ideas as a whole class. This form of organisation provides the most supportive arrangement initially for children to express ideas (a familiar partner), but then challenges groups progressively to explain their thoughts to others, assimilate other groups' approaches and perhaps modify their own views as a result, though a consensus position is not the necessary outcome.

Jigsawing

Here 'home' groups of five or six are set up to consider the chosen topic for discussion. Each child in the 'home' group is then given one particular aspect of the topic to investigate and to inform the rest of the group about later. The appropriate children from the 'home' groups then form into 'expert' groupings consisting of those children investigating the same aspect of the topic (e.g. game shows in a discussion about children's television). The 'experts' eventually return to their 'home' groups where they report on their deliberations so far. Further research might be done by the individual 'experts' in the classroom, school library or at home, and further 'expert' meetings might take place until eventually the 'home' group draws together all its expert contributions into a report or possibly a wall display for the whole class.

The use of these two groups allows each child to have a definite role to play within the 'home' grouping, enabling them to 'don the mantle of the expert' whilst they brief this group, and avoiding the problem of having 'passengers' within discussion groups.

Rainbowing

All the members of a group are given a colour or a number. After a period spent in discussion, all children with the same colour or number form new groups to recount what they have talked about thus far.

This should ensure that all children have something to contribute to their second group at least. It also means that children work with a variety of other pupils as speakers and listeners and not only with regular partners or groups.

Envoying

Groups are allowed to send 'envoys' at certain times to other groups to explain their ideas, enquire about progress in the tasks in hand, get responses and suggestions. 'Envoys' might also be sent to obtain information from the school library or teacher, as agreed, and then report back.

'Envoys' might be particularly appropriate in drama activities where the groups represent, say, neighbouring villages or competing companies. This kind of organisation gives the groups more independence of the teacher and allows for inter-group activity.

Part of planning and organising oracy for the primary teacher will be the careful monitoring of the frequency and type of pupils' experience of speaking and listening across the curriculum. A grid reproduced here from *The Primary Language Record: Handbook for Teachers* (ILEA, 1988 p.38) could serve this monitoring purpose well:

	SOCIAL CONTEXTS			
LEARNING CONTEXTS	pair	small group	child with adult	small/large group with adult
collaborative reading and writing activities				
play, dramatic play, drama & storying				
environmental studies & historical research				
maths & science investigations				
design, construction, craft & art projects				

Using this or a similar framework, possibly mapping audience where appropriate onto the grid, it is possible to check at a glance that pupils are encountering a range of situations, audiences and activities. Without such a checking system, work in oracy can soon become identified by pupils with one particular curriculum subject or area and with one particular group or kind of grouping, and teachers may be unaware of their own particular biases.

Assessment of speaking and listening

To English falls the main responsibility within the National Curriculum for monitoring and assessing children's development as speakers and listeners. Athough the majority of oral work may take place in other curriculum contexts, it is in relation to English AT1 that pupils' achievements in oracy as such will be measured. The Working Group which produced the 1989 English curriculum fought hard for AT1 to be given the equal weighting it has with Reading and with Writing at KS 1 and 2 in the overall assessment of English in the National Curriculum (Cox, 1992).

Speaking and listening is certainly the most difficult of the three English profile components to assess. There is usually no tangible outcome on which assessment can be based, unless taping is used. Skills and competencies in oral work are often demonstrated in the process of producing other outcomes — such as solving a Maths problem or carrying out a Science experiment — which may also be assessed for other purposes. Objective assessment is always problematic where the teacher too is involved in the process as a speaker and listener, a player rather than an umpire. The special context-bound nature of assessment in speaking and listening is recognised in the National Curriculum by the fact that there have been no Standard Assessment Tests (SATs) for English AT1 and the levels of achievement of pupils have been decided by teachers' own records only. Suggested guidelines were made available, however, to primary teachers to promote a more standardised approach to teacher assessment of speaking and listening in line with the suggestions of the English Working Group (SEAC, 1991a and b).

The main recommendation of that Group was that the assessment of oracy should 'where possible, be informal, continuous and incidental, applied to tasks carried out for curricular purposes.' For them, this ruled out the systematic use of tape-recording since it would not be 'part of normal classroom activity' unless specifically planned into a task by the teacher (Cox, 1989 para. 15.42). The major source of information, therefore, for the teacher, will be planned observations of pupils in small numbers, as they are participating in various speaking and listening activities as outlined above.

Written comments arising from these observations will need to note the social and learning contexts in which the activities took place, and of course be dated. They will also need to be made within the framework of English AT1 which provides a set of criteria against which development in oracy must be measured for National Curriculum reporting purposes. These criteria take the form of Level Descriptions which contain four strands of oracy development, related to the three main contexts for developing oral skills mentioned earlier:

(i)   Children's ability to participate as speakers and listeners in a group or whole class activities (e.g. role-play, discussion).

(ii) Children's ability to listen attentively and respond to what they hear (e.g. responding to literature, receiving instructions and messages).

(iii) Children's ability to communicate with the teacher, other adults or pupils, or the whole class (e.g. reporting, giving a presentation).

The Level Descriptions are intended as holistic statements of children's attainment. Teachers choose whichever description ' best fits' the child's stage of development, even if not all the strands within it have been achieved. However it is helpful to separate out the four strands for the purposes of looking at progression. Of the 8 levels for English, levels 1-3 will apply to the great majority of pupils at KS1 and levels 2-5 at KS2. However since 'each description should be considered in conjunction with the descriptions for adjacent levels' (p.17), levels 1-6 are included here:

AT1 SPEAKING AND LISTENING: LEVEL DESCRIPTIONS

Statements emphasising the development of talk:
level 1: Pupils talk about matters of immediate interest.

level 2: Pupils begin to show confidence in talking and listening , particularly where the topics interest them. In developing and explaining their ideas they speak clearly and use a growing vocabulary.

level 3: Pupils talk and listen confidently in different contexts, exploring and communicating ideas.

level 4: Pupils talk and listen with confidence in an increasing range of contexts.

level 5: Pupils talk and listen confidently in a wide range of contexts, including some that are of a formal nature.

level 6: Pupils adapt their talk to the demands of different contexts with increasing confidence.

Statements emphasising the development of listening:
level 1: They listen to others and usually respond appropriately.

level 2: They usually listen carefully and respond with increasing appropriateness to what others say.

level 3: Through relevant comments and questions, they show they have listened carefully.

level 4: In discussion, they listen carefully, making contributions and asking questions that are responsive to others' ideas and views.

level 5: In discussion, they pay close attention to what others say, ask questions to develop ideas and make contributions that take account of others' views.

level 6: Pupils take an active part in discussion, showing understanding of ideas and sensitivity to others.

Developing a sense of audience and purpose:
level 1: They convey simple meanings to a range of listeners, speaking audibly, and begin to extend their ideas and accounts by providing some detail.

level 2: On occasions, they show awareness of the needs of the listener by including relevant detail.

level 3: They begin to adapt what they say to the needs of the listener, varying the use of vocabulary and the level of detail.

level 4: Their talk is adapted to the purpose: developing ideas thoughtfully, describing events and conveying their opinions clearly.

level 5 : Their talk engages the interest of the listener as they begin to vary their expression and vocabulary.

level 6: Their talk engages the interest of the listener through the variety of its vocabulary and expression.

Developing awareness and use of standard English:
level 1: [no reference]

level 2: They are beginning to be aware that in some situations a more formal vocabulary and tone of voice are used.

level 3: They are beginning to be aware of standard English and when it is used.

level 4: They use appropriately some of the features of standard English vocabulary and grammar.

level 5: They begin to use standard English in formal situations.

level 6: They are usually fluent in their use of standard English in formal situations.

A planned weekly programme of observation of a small number of pupils in the course of normal classroom activities should allow the teacher to measure development in oracy against many of these criteria. But it will be necessary from time to time to organise activities deliberately, so as to give particular children the opportunity to engage with one or more tasks suggested by the programmes of study and level descriptions.

Selective use of audio and video taping as part of speaking and listening activities (e.g. radio plays, making a video for younger children), will also occasionally provide samples which will allow more considered assessment to back up classroom observations. In addition, planned conversations, or 'conferences', with individual pupils or small groups will provide occasions when children can convey their own perception of their achievements. Many teachers meet the requirement of the NC that 'pupils should be taught to evaluate their own talk and reflect on how it varies' (p.11), by using prompt sheets or questionnaires to elicit written self-assessment from children before such conversations. Comments can often be honest and revealing, like this one from a Y6 boy:

Talking & Listening

I could have listened more. But when I talked it allways seemed to be at the wrong time I think it is quite hard talking in a group because everyone talks at the same time unless you have a very copretive group I think I may be a bit bossy in a group.

As with all assessment, information gained through these procedures can serve different purposes and audiences at different times. Two main functions stand out: summative and formative.

Observations and samples of children as speakers and listeners need to be used formatively by teachers themselves as an integral part of a cycle of planning, organising and monitoring oracy for the whole class. Records of children's achievements should *inform* and modify teaching plans not only in English but across the whole curriculum. For individual children or groups of children, assessment in oracy will serve the diagnostic purpose of determining what they have so far achieved and therefore what the next step is they need to take.

The same information, probably in a different format, will need to be used summatively at various points in the school year and in children's school career, to 'sum up' how they are performing and 'where they are' in terms of the National Curriculum levels and possibly in terms of norms for a given age group. Here the audience being served will, of course, be different: not teachers themselves but parents, other teachers or other schools.

Further Reading

Howe, A. and Johnson, J. (1992) [eds] *Common Bonds: Storytelling in the Classroom.* London: Hodder and Stoughton.

Howe, A. (1992) *Making Talk Work.* London: Hodder and Stoughton.

NOP (1991) *Teaching Talking and Learning in KS2.* York: NCC.

Norman, K. (1990)*Teaching Talking and Learning in KS1.* York: NCC.

Norman, K. (1992) *Thinking Voices.* London: Hodder and Stoughton.

Chapter Two

READING

The Background

> Let us ... express our conclusion at the outset in plain terms: there is
> no one method, medium, approach, device or philosophy that holds
> the key to the process of learning to read. We believe that the
> knowledge does exist to improve the teaching of reading, but that it
> does not lie in the triumphant discovery, or re-discovery, of a
> particular formula ... The main arguments about how reading should
> be taught have been repeated over and over again as the decades pass,
> but the problems remain (p.77).

The Bullock Committee of Inquiry which came to this conclusion was set
up by the then Education Secretary, Margaret Thatcher, in 1972 at a time
of public concern about reading standards. At the very beginning of their
report, the Committee pointed to parallels with the situation at the time of
the Newbolt Report of 1921, when there was similar public anxiety,
particularly from employers, about lower standards of literacy (p.3).
Recently we have seen the 'great debate' about standards in reading
revived and the main arguments 'repeated over and over again' with
renewed force during the creation and implementation of a National
Curriculum for English. With each committee of inquiry and each debate

in the press and on television, there has been popular expectation that 'a panacea can be found that will make everything right' (p.77) with the teaching of the 'first R'. It is worth reiterating at the start that no such magic formula exists nor can exist because of the unique complexity of the act of reading.

When we read we engage in a highly sophisticated process which integrates a whole complex of different knowledge, skills and under-standing about language. To a literate adult the act of reading feels like a single experience, as apparently effortless as breathing. The practised ease with which we devour print disguises the way in which we are instantaneously processing and unifying diverse sources of data both on the page and within our own minds as we read (as you read this, for example). Making a list of all the reading done during any one day will also reveal the diversity of texts we read and the great variety of personal and social contexts for reading most of us experience.

Four main sources within written language provide us with the important threads we weave together into the seamless experience of reading. These are the four Ss:

- *sense*: the system of meaning, or semantics, both at the level of words and the level of larger units of discourse

- *syntax*: the system of ordering words, phrases, clauses and sentences into meaningful patterns, sometimes called 'grammar'

- *sight*: the system of conventionalised symbols, or graphology, which appears on the page

- *sound*: the system of meaningful sounds, or phonology, which makes up our spoken language

If we are fluent readers we must be handling *all* these different systems within written language simultaneously, although we may vary in how much emphasis we give to each one. (For example, do you tend to 'sound' the words in your head as you read this? Do you sub-vocalise in your throat? Or is your reading completely 'silent'?)

The main arguments which have been repeated over the past decades have concentrated on two different views of what reading is and therefore how it should be taught, views which tend to attach greater importance to some of the systems within written language than to others. These two views could be described as:

- one which sees reading as mainly concerned with phonic and with graphic awareness

- another which sees it as to do pre-eminently with meaning and with language structure

The two concepts of the reading process are often referred to as using 'bottom-up' and 'top-down' models respectively (see, for example, Wray and Medwell, 1991).

The 'bottom-up' model is so called because the act of reading is conceived as a type of code-breaking exercise where it is necessary first to decipher individual letters, words or sounds, and then to move systematically upwards from this basis, by building letters and sounds into words or words into sentences and sentences into larger units of print, and so on to arrive at meaning. The 'top-down 'model, sometimes called a psycholinguistic one, begins within the mind of the individual reader and its capacity to make meaning from the experience of print. In this model, reading involves the mind sampling print selectively, predicting and hypothesising, drawing on implicit knowledge about language structure, but not processing separately every individual letter, sound or even word on the page.

Children learning to read

Each of these views of what is involved in reading leads to a different approach to the teaching of reading in the primary classroom. Firstly, the bottom-up model is identified with what are sometimes called behaviourist approaches, emphasising step-by-step instruction in a set of discrete skills concerned with the processing of letter sounds or word shapes.

The Phonics Method

The starting point in this method is for children to learn the sounds to which written letters correspond, beginning with the initial sounds of familiar words and moving on, say, to final sounds, consonant blends and digraphs. Traditional phonic training uses rote-learning to instil in beginning readers the individual letter sounds which make up words: 'kuh-ah-tuh' for CAT and so on. More recent phonics, recognising that in fact the individual sounds above do not say the word CAT as we pronounce it, tend to concentrate more on larger units of sound in words, breaking up the above into 'kuh-at', for example (the 'rime' and 'onset', as they are known — see Bryant, 1994). The use of games, rhymes and other activities have replaced learning by heart and whole-class chanting in more modern phonics teaching.

The drawbacks to phonics, leaving aside theoretical considerations about the nature of reading and of learning which may accompany it, lie in the structure of the English language itself. An alphabet of 26 letters (or graphemes) has to represent on the page 44 different sounds (phonemes) which speakers of standard English produce. Inevitably this means that some letters or combinations of letters have to represent more than one sound, for example the 'ea' combination in:

meat   break   threat

To compound the difficulty there is an inherent irregularity which means that sometimes the same sounds are represented by different letter combinations, for examples the 'fuh' sound in:

fun   enough   phone

Linguis its describe English as not having a complete phoneme- grapheme correspondence, although there are obviously many regular patterns of sounds and spellings within the language. For this reason, relying on phonic information alone to process text will lead to confusion and frustration unless the reading materials used are, like children's phonic readers, highly controlled and artificial in vocabulary and syntax. Nevertheless it is clear that general phonological awareness and some specific phonic skills are important for children in their early encounters with meaningful print and that these are stimulated by the very earliest children's literature, nursery rhymes and songs.

The Look and Say Method

Here the emphasis is upon training children's response to the visual features of whole words. Sometimes knows as 'word recognition', this method involves children building up a 'sight vocabulary' of words they can immediately say when they encounter them in written form. Visual memory is trained by techniques such as the use of 'flash cards', cards containing complete common words which the teachers 'flashes' up in front of pupils for a short time, saying or asking the children to say the word represented. This method shares with traditional phonics a teacher-led rote-learning procedure in the classroom. 'Look and say' begins slightly further from the bottom of the language system than phonics, starting with whole words or even with sentences in extensions of this method, but in practice it is more behaviourist relying heavily on conditioned responses to the 'flash card' or similar stimulus.

The disadvantages of 'look and say' reside in its reliance on this stimulus-response learning style. Children's lack of understanding not just of word meanings but of any idea of reading as a meaning-making activity can easily be hidden behind the rehearsed response to the familiar word card (or to the ink-stain in its corner!). Whereas, in time, phonics can equip children with the skills to 'attack' and de-code unknown words (overtones of warfare here!), 'look and say' does require a dependence on the teacher for the learning of new words. Like phonics it can restrict children's early reading texts to uninteresting primers with heavily restricted vocabularies. Over-reliance on the visual clues of whole words will also lead to frustration if other skills and concepts are not acquired before 'real' texts are encountered. Nevertheless all readers need to acquire a sight vocabulary of common words from books and from their own experience, which they can process semi-automatically, if they are to become fluent readers. The shape of words is also an important cue at the level of their outline profile on the page: any difference in length or in the pattern of ascenders and descenders as in, say, 'shape' (⊏⊐⊏⊐) and 'spade' (⊏⊐⊏⊐).

The other view of reading, which highlights the importance of the reader rather than that of the code or text, has given rise to alternative approaches (not strictly speaking 'methods') in the primary classroom.

The Real Books Approach

This phrase is used since it is the popular tag, as are 'phonics' and 'look and say', although all three have acquired pejorative connotations in the acrimonious reading standards debate. The 'real books' in question are sometimes called trade books, the commercially produced individual works of children's authors which are the rich reading resource this approach has brought into a central place in the primary classroom, to replace or supplement the reading scheme texts used in the previous two methods.

Behind the use of 'real books' is a belief in the capacity of even beginner readers to create meanings from texts: meaning is, in fact, seen to reside not in the code on the page but in the mind of the reader who processes it. For this reason, it is seen as imperative that the books which children encounter in their introduction to reading should be rewarding in terms of interest, attractiveness and enjoyment. Examples of such texts are the young children's picture books which in the past twenty-five years have evolved into an exciting new genre of children's (and now adult) literature. Advocates of this psycholinguistic approach to reading see the authors of such books as actually the best teachers of reading today, since they motivate children to join 'the literacy club' and allow them to 'learn to read by reading' (Meek, 1988, Smith, 1985).

In the classroom this approach is often organised in an 'apprenticeship' structure. This form of organisation treats pupils as apprentice readers learning the craft of reading (that is, not just decoding skills but the ability to make sense of and take pleasure from complete texts) in the workshop of a master reader, the teacher, another adult or other children, by actually reading worthwhile books. Children have a wider choice of reading material than when restricted to reading scheme texts. Sometimes a system known as 'individualised reading' is used to provide guidance on the level of reading difficulty of real books as well as scheme books (Moon, 1995). Books are shared with an interested adult (teacher, helper or parent) or with more fluent children until readers reach independence. This approach does not exclude learning about the shape and sounds of words but sets this learning in the context of the pursuit of worthwhile meaning. There is no ladder of skills acquisition to climb, though, before that pursuit can begin.

The disadvantages of this holistic approach to learning to read lie in its apparently unstructured nature which can make monitoring of development more difficult. Followed in its pure form (as it never would be in practice) it could leave children lacking in the skills needed to cope with unfamiliar text without the support of an interested adult. It is based on the way in which most children first encounter books at home, reading with an adult carer, and usually involves the integration of this parental activity, known as 'shared reading', into the school's reading programme. Some children, of course, will not enjoy the benefits of a home environment where books are shared in this way and may not respond to this approach in school. However, it is clear that without appreciation of the many uses and pleasures associated with reading real books children are less likely to become readers in the fullest sense of the word.

The Language Experience Approach

This shares with the last a holistic approach to literacy learning, sometimes called a 'whole language' approach, which emphasises the links between all aspects of children's language, speech, reading and writing, and seeks to integrate them in practice. Its starting point is slightly further down the language system since it begins with children's own spoken language. Typically children learn to read initially simple texts which they compose or dictate themselves.

The *Breakthrough to Literacy* materials (Mackay et al, 1979), most closely connected with a language experience approach, enable pupils to compose text using sentence makers (a bit like Scrabble letter-holders) on which are placed together word cards either ready printed or written by the teacher on demand. New words can also be constructed from individual letter cards. Thus children's initial reading is of familiar, meaningful texts. They are able to read what they can say themselves, both seeing what it looks like in print and hearing its sounds also.

Links with children's spoken language are naturally made, but it is not assumed that children will learn to read in the same way they learn to speak, as sometimes claimed for psycholinguistic approaches. There is a more structured and systematic procedure involved here. Attention is drawn to both letter patterns and whole word shapes but the emphasis, certainly in more recent forms of the language experience approach, is not on word or letter recognition but on the creation of meaning and on the exploitation of children's implicit knowledge about language structure, especially syntax.

Limitations of the language experience approach again involve the restricted nature of the texts children tend to create and encounter as reading material. Although *Breakthrough to Literacy* originally also involved the use of a set of graded reading books, there is still the need for transition from limited, speech-based texts to the individual experience of real books, which is the end of all reading teaching. Children will need to realise eventually that there are significant qualitative differences between spoken and written language and that fluent reading involves developing an awareness of those differences.

This (much simplified) outline has revealed two main views of what reading is and four main methods of, or approaches to, teaching initial reading. The next thing to say is that it would be unusual to find an actual classroom where either of those views in extreme form was followed or any of those methods or approaches was used exclusively. They are distinguished in this way for the sake of drawing a conceptual sketch map of reading teaching. In practice most primary teachers, intuitively arriving at the considered conclusion of the Bullock committee and of the most recent reseach (Bryant, 1995), use a mixture of some or all of the above ways of teaching reading. This is because classroom teachers soon realise that in any group of pupils some will respond to one approach, some to another; that different skills, knowledge and experiences are needed at different stages of reading development; and that in fact all readers need to employ *a variety of strategies* in learning and developing reading. Research has confirmed the importance of the teacher as perhaps the single most influential factor in children's learning to read. Reading failure is more likely to occur in classrooms where teachers adhere rigidly to one method or approach only and individual children employ one strategy only in their increasingly frustrating encounters with print.

The history of reading teaching shows different views and approaches in the ascendancy at different periods. The oldest method of teaching reading is actually the 'alphabetic', not used in primary schools today, which consists of pupils learning the code of the letter names. Children presumably learnt to read their Biblical texts despite this 'method' rather than because of it.

Old-style phonics is often referred to as the 'traditional' primary method. Introduced in the mid-nineteenth century, it supplanted the alphabetic method by the early twentieth and was widely used in the 1920s and 30s. 'Look and say' methods became popular in the 1940s and 50s as a result of dissatisfaction with phonics, though it is important to appreciate that there was not (and never has been) any wholesale abandonment of phonic methods and different methods continued to be used side by side (Beard, 1987). Psycholinguistic concepts of reading have influenced reading teaching since the 1960s and throughout the 70s and 80s. *Breakthrough to Literacy*, as a set of materials, was published in 1970 and followed developmental work on the application of linguistics to English teaching. Since then it has been widely used in primary schools.

The 1989 *English in the National Curriculum* was based on a broad view of reading which emphasised meaning:

> Reading is much more than the decoding of black marks upon a page: it is a quest for meaning and one which requires the reader to be an active participant. (Cox, 1989 para 16.2).

In terms of teaching, a holistic approach is recommended whilst recognising the need stressed by Bullock to avoid over-reliance on any one method:

> In their quest for meaning, children need to be helped to become confident and resourceful in the use of a variety of reading cues. They need to be able to recognise on sight a large proportion of the words they encounter and to be able to predict meaning on the basis of phonic, idiomatic and grammatical regularities and of what makes sense in context; children should be encouraged to make informed guesses. Teachers should recognise that reading is a complex but unitary process and not a set of discrete skills which can be taught separately in turn and, ultimately, bolted together (para 16.9).

The 1995 revisions to AT2 are influenced by the increased interest shown in recent reading research, mostly conducted from the standpoint of cognitive and developmental psychology, in phonological awareness in children as an important factor in learning to read (e.g. Bryant and Bradley, 1985). This shift of interest has led to a parallel resurgence of popularity in phonic methods of teaching (see Adams, 1990), though, like skills-based approaches to English generally, these have never actually disappeared from classrooms. However the 1995 programmes of study emphasise, in terms of 'Range', that 'pupils should be given extensive experience of children's literature' and that ' materials read and discussed should be used to stimulate pupils' imagination and enthusiasm' (p.6). There is also a stress in terms of 'Key Skills' on a 'balanced and coherent programme' (p.7) which should include knowledge, understanding and skills in the four areas mentioned earlier:

Contextual understanding (Sense)
Grammatical knowledge (Syntax)
Graphic knowledge and Word recognition (Sight)
Phonic knowledge (Sound)

The approach is summed up in this way:

Pupils should be taught to read with fluency, accuracy, understanding and enjoyment, building on what they already know. In order to help them develop understanding of the nature and purpose of reading, they should be given an extensive introduction to books, stories and words in print around them. Pupils should be taught the alphabet, and be made aware of the sounds of spoken language in order to develop phonological awareness. They should also be taught to use various approaches to word identification and recognition, and to use their understanding of grammatical structure and the meaning of the text as a whole to make sense of print. (p.6)

Developing Reading

Whilst debate has raged over the initial teaching and learning of reading, there has until recently been a comparative neglect of the development of children's reading once they have become independent readers, by whatever methods. The Bullock Report was the first official inquiry to look beyond initial reading and was followed shortly afterwards by two Schools Council projects in the mid-1970s, *Extending Beginning Reading* (Southgate et al, 1981) which looked at the reading of 7-9 year olds, and *The Effective Use of Reading* (Lunzer and Gardner, 1979) which studied 10-15 year olds' educational reading. However recently published HMI reports and studies of the implementation of the National Curriculum have expressed concern still that independent readers at KS2 are too frequently left without the support of a programme specifically designed to develop their skills further (for example, HMI, 1990 para 52).

The 1995 NC addresses these concerns by requiring that children be given opportunities 'to develop as enthusiastic, independent and reflective readers' at KS2:

> They should be introduced to a wide range of literature, and have opportunities to read extensively for their own interest and pleasure, and for information. Pupils' reading should be developed through the use of progressively more challenging and demanding texts. Opportunities for reading should include both independent and shared reading of play scripts and other texts, by groups and the whole class (p.13).

At KS2, or after children have become 'free' readers, development will concentrate on increasing the range and complexity of types of writing children encounter, including information books as well as fiction and poetry, and on deepening and making more effective their response to and understanding of all these texts. Reading of and response to a range of literature and the increasing ability to use research skills in the classroom and library will need to be part of a coherent reading policy.

Let's look now at reading development in action in the primary classroom.

Reading in the Classroom

A Y4 class are settling down to their daily reading time. It's half an hour at the end of the morning today, since their teacher does not like this slot to be always left until the last part of the day, as often happens. The settling down involves the children arranging themselves into seven teacher-selected groups of four and sharing out within their groups copies of the short novels they are reading. Each group has copies of a different book. The books are:

Bernard Ashley	*I'm Trying to Tell You*
Jeff Brown	*Flat Stanley*
Roald Dahl	*Fantastic Mr Fox*
Ted Hughes	*The Iron Man*

Shirley Isherwood	*William's Problems*
Jan Mark	*The Dead Letter Box*
Jill Tomlinson	*The Owl Who Was Afraid of the Dark*

The groups are of mixed reading ability but the children are skilled in sharing out the reading appropriately within their group. So each child usually takes it in turn to read aloud for a few minutes or until a natural break in the text occurs. Some of the groups, at the teacher's suggestion, have organised the reading so that each reader has the part of a character or characters within the story, with one child as narrator. The groups are keeping in mind the teacher's reminder that they must read in such a way that all their own group can hear them clearly but the other groups cannot. The teacher has taken the narrator's part in one group which contains two children with particular difficulties in reading and so is able to support these non-fluent readers both in their listening, responding and reading aloud.

When the groups finish their reading, they will be given time to discuss their impressions of the book as a group. This sharing of immediate responses and coming to a more considered view of a book through talk is one of the most valuable aspects of this type of reading organisation. The teacher will provide a list of initial questions to be considered about the novel read, using the categories suggested by Bentley and Rowe (1991 see p.8 and p.24):

• questions about the story itself

• questions about the illustrations

• questions about the way the story has been written

In a future session, when discussion about the book is completed, groups will report their reactions to their reading to the rest of the class. Eventually all the groups will have read all the seven books and commented on them in this way. It hardly needs pointing out how this group reading activity dovetails with the promotion of oracy outlined in Chapter One, as well as with recent reseach suggesting the value of collaborative reading (Gorman et al, 1994) reflected in the 1995 NC requirements above.

This is by no means the only reading time this class enjoys during a typical week. Since the teacher has a strong belief in the value of literature in the classroom and takes every opportunity to organise book-based activities, reading has a generous allocation of time and space. Each day, at the start of afternoon school, a period of Uninterrupted Sustained Silent Reading (USSR) takes place. Everyone in the school reads, including the teachers (even reputedly the caretaker!) for twenty minutes. Books for this silent reading time are selected by the children themselves from the class book corner, school library or from home. Twice a week paired reading is also organised at this time. This involves pupils from a Y6 class in the school pairing up with less confident readers from the Y4 class to share their reading. The pairs can read aloud together, or one or the other pupil can take a turn to read. There is also time to talk about the book in question. At this time the remaining Y4 children can also pair up if they wish and share books in this way.

The children keep an individual record of books which they read at this time, recording details of author, title, when started and finished, and a brief comment on their reading. For books which they feel they particularly enjoyed, they can choose a book review sheet from a variety of different designs and complete a review to be placed in a class book-file. This file is kept in the book corner for all the class to consult when they are selecting reading material. This corner holds the classroom's collection of fiction, poetry and non-fiction. The books have been colour-coded to give a guide to the level of reading difficulty, but the children have arranged the books themselves on the shelves. There are posters and book jackets, some created by the children, on the walls and bookcases and carpet and comfortable cushions to sit on. The children take it in turns to look after the corner and keep it tidy. Sometimes the teacher sits in this area to talk to individual children or to small groups about their reading and to listen to them reading aloud.

When the class are not engaged in group reading tasks, the teacher tends to use that time-slot to read aloud to them from a variety of texts. Most commonly this will be a class novel, chosen because it is worth listening to and talking about and because it represents a literary experience just beyond what most of the children could manage in their own reading. However, it might also be a short story, traditional tales from around the world or a selection of poems. Equally it could be a non-narrative text, a book of argument or information, chosen to fit in with an aspect of classroom work or because it is topical. The teacher believes that it is important for the pupils to hear worthwhile non-fiction read aloud and for them to have opportunities to talk about it and respond to it also.

As part of their History Study Unit on 'Life in Tudor times' the children are also using non-fiction texts from the classroom and school library. Sometimes group reading and discussion of extracts from information books takes place, with structured activities for the groups to complete (see the section on Directed Activities Related to Texts below). At other times children are researching alone or in pairs. The teacher encourages them first of all to make a list of questions they want to answer through their reading. Library skills of finding a book through use of a cataloguing system, using encyclopaedias and other reference material, and study skills such as using contents and indexes are practised in a real context.

The 'Life in Tudor times' unit also provides a historical context for encountering Shakespeare and his work. The class have read about the theatre of Shakespeare's time, constructed model theatres, read Leon Garfield's abridgement of *Romeo and Juliet* (1993) and watched an animated film version of it (BBC TV, 1992).

This sketch of classroom practice at KS2 highlights the two main aspects of reading development beyond initial reading skills: reading and responding to literature and information-retrieval for the purposes of study. These now need to be considered in more detail.

Reading and Responding to Literature

The Newbolt report in 1921 argued for 'reading' to be transformed to 'literature' in the elementary school syllabus after a certain stage. This was at a period when there was certainly a sharp divide between the 'primer' texts children encountered as their first reading material and the 'great literature' they were expected to go on to encounter. The increase in the quantity as well as the quality of children's literature in English in the last forty years now means that encounters with genuine literature can begin for children with their very earliest experience of individual, authored books. Children's authors such as Leon Garfield can also make 'great literature' appropriately accessible for younger readers. The distinction between 'reading' and 'literature' is therefore much less relevant when the development of reading is viewed as a continuous process leading into adult life.

Responding to literature likewise has its origins in initial listening to, reading and talking about stories and poems in the KS1 classroom, as is recognised in both 1989 and 1995 versions of AT2. It is certainly not a case of learning to read and then learning to read literature or practise 'literary appreciation' or the like. Understanding and responding to texts will also involve something more than traditional comprehension work. Response to fiction or poetry texts, read individually, in a pair, a group or as a whole class, might, for example, take any of these practical forms:

- acting out scenes from a traditional tale

- performing a poem

- designing publicity material for a book

- making a radio or video version of an extract from a novel

- writing in the role of a character from a story

- making an anthology of poems on the same theme or by the same poets

- preparing stories or extracts to read to a younger audience

All of these response activities, properly pursued, involve children not only 'reading the lines', but also 'reading between the lines', making inferences and deductions from what they read, and sometimes 'reading beyond the lines', making evaluations and justifying their own personal views of what they read (see Benton and Fox, 1985 and Cairney, 1990 for further activities). Before a poem can be effectively performed, for example, pupils need to look closely, with teacher support, at how it is written, how its various parts fit together, any effects of sound or visual patterning, voices used, meanings conveyed and so forth. At this stage of development (and probably at later KS too) a creative response such as this which brings in the full range of children's language and literacy skills, rather than a purely written exercise involving the answering of set questions, is much more productive.

Response activities of this type need not be seen as vague or unstructured. A theoretical back-bone is provided, for example, by Benton and Fox (1985 pp. 13-16) who list 'four activities that comprise the basic elements of the process of responding':

- *picturing*, or the making of mental images

- *anticipating and retrospecting*, a continuous series of predictions and backward glances

- *interacting*, which involves the reader projecting into the text his or her own experience

- *evaluating*, the valuing of a text which also goes on continuously as one reads

These processes are all present and interrelate in the act of reading literature. However, it is possible for teachers to devise activities which highlight one or other of these elements of response. Benton and Fox suggest:

i) **Picturing**

Pupils can be asked to jot down their expectations before starting to read a book, based on the visual stimulus of the cover. Thumb-nail sketches can be made of characters, places or incidents in a story, particularly to give first impressions when they appear. Doodling or jotting could go on during reading! More considered pictures or perhaps collages can be created to express responses after reading a book.

ii) **Anticipating and Retrospecting**

A frieze of plot development for display in the classroom, to be updated regularly, can both tap into this process and stimulate it further. Diaries and letters written in the role of characters will involve children in deliberately looking forward and backwards in texts. Encouraging pupils to keep a reading journal or log to be completed after each reading session will make prediction and retrospection easier.

iii) **Interacting**

Improvised drama and role-play activities provide opportunities for children both to put themselves into the action of a story, play or poem, and make the action relevant to themselves as individuals. Writing imaginary incidents using the same characters can also encourage the interplay of reader and text.

iv) *Evaluating*

Planning an advertising campaign for a book; writing a letter to the author; tape-recording or videoing a Book Programme or Desert Island Books are all activities which prompt pupils to articulate the evaluative responses they are making as they read.

Picture Books

A programme of reading development at KS2 needs both to widen children's experience of reading all kinds of texts and also to provide opportunities for the full range of response activities suggested above. Clearly this will be a programme which develops the whole of children's language, speaking, listening and writing as well as reading.

A good example of this integrated approach to developing wide reading and full response to literature involves experience of the contemporary picture books mentioned earlier. An effective way to explore these mixed media texts with older primary pupils (Y5/6) is to have as an outcome of their extended reading of and reflection on them the production of their own picture book for younger children (say, Y2). This will involve pupils reading individually or as a pair examples of picture books by authors whose work is attractive and accessible to the whole primary age range, such as (to name just a few):

Janet and Allan Ahlberg
Anthony Browne
John Burningham
Shirley Hughes
Satoshi Kitamura
David McKee
Maurice Sendak

These books will need to be shared and talked about in small groups ('how do we read them? words or pictures first?') and previous experiences of picture books mentioned ('babies' books', 'learning to read books'). Teacher intervention at this stage can point the children towards investigating the relationship between words and pictures ('which came first?', 'what happens if you take one away?'). A useful activity here is to ask pupils to provide the missing text for a series of pictures taken from a book, or to supply pictures to accompany a given simple text. Attention can then be directed towards the pictures and the aesthetic effects achieved by different artists using different styles. Jane Doonan's work in this area is a revelation for many teachers (Doonan, 1993).

Out of their wide reading of picture books and as a response to them and an exploration of the genre, children can then work in pairs on creating their own picture books, possibly telling a familiar story. This will involve careful consideration of how such texts work and informed decisions about, for example, text and picture balance and layout, as well as reading difficulty, all within a real and purposeful context.

Once created the picture books can then be read aloud by their authors and shown to their intended younger audience, thus completing the cycle of reading experience with which the activity began. Loaned to the class library of these younger pupils, the picture books can be read and shared by individual children whose responses in turn can be recorded and fed back to the authors. Children learn a great deal about the process of reading and the relationship between authors, readers and texts from their experience of writing for this kind of listener and reader. Skills and understanding in Art and Design and Technology are also being developed alongside these.

Poems

Poetry is often regarded as the icing on the cake of children's literary experience (if not the decoration on the top) rather than the essential ingredient it can be. Surveys have revealed its comparative popularity with primary age children in contrast to secondary pupils (APU, 1981, 1982). For less fluent readers it is frequently a popular choice and a rare experience of enjoyable literature. In this case the rhythm and repetitive sound and word patterns provide a valuable support to inexperienced readers (Lockwood, 1993). Poetry's role in stimulating phonological awareness has been recognised in recent reading schemes such as the *Oxford Reading Tree* and Ginn's *All Aboard*.

Children's poetry reading should initially link with their early experiences of poetic language. So a natural starting point might be to collect and display examples of:

dips	puns
riddles	advertising jingles
playground chants	slogans
mnemonics	song lyrics
hymns	greetings cards

as well as of the published poems children know. Having built a bridge from where children are, taking them further means adding to their existing, and mostly unrealised repertoire of poetry, new experiences in reading and, of course, writing and speaking and listening to poetry, since the three will always overlap in practice.

Opportunities to browse through a variety of up-to-date poetry books, dip into them, share and discuss what they find are essential. There has never been a greater quantity or quality of children's poetry published than over the past thirty years. Many well-known poets write for children as often as for adults including Charles Causley, Roger McGough, Brian Patten and, of course, the Poet Laureate Ted Hughes. A revolution in poetry for children in English was initiated when Michael Rosen published *Mind Your Own Business* in 1974. For the first time the voice and the thoughts of the urban, state-school child could be heard in Rosen's free verse. Many others have successfully followed that lead using many different voices: Kit Wright, Gareth Owen, Allan Ahlberg, for instance. Others such as John Mole and Richard Edwards, have continued the more traditional poetic craft of earlier children's poets like Walter de la Mare or James Reeves. In the 1980s the voices of Black English have been heard in children's poetry for the first time, talking of alternative childhood experiences in the works of John Agard, James Berry, Grace Nichols and others.

With many poems, reading, sharing and talking will be enough. Experiencing poetry need not lead to analysing it in the way which alienates many secondary pupils later. Where it is appropriate, responding to poems further might take one of these forms:

- investigating the characters and incidents behind poems

- making a board game based on a longer poem
  (e.g. a ballad or other narrative poem)

- using well-known poems as models for imitation
  ('The Tyger') or parody ('Daffodils')

- choral speaking of a poem, where the whole class takes part like a choir or chorus.

Acitivities such as group reading and discussion of poetry and poetry performances have already been mentioned. In the end the most important factor in this area of reading development will again be the individual teacher. She or he will need to communicate enthusiasm for the magic of poetry rather than anxiety about the mystification which often surrounds it.

Information Retrieval

The original English Working Group of 1989 proposed that this aspect of children's reading development, sometimes called 'reading for learning', should form a separate AT. However, consultation with teachers and others persuaded them that reading for information in this way was not a different kind of reading but rather a further development of initial reading skills in response to the demands of different kinds of texts.

The 1995 NC consistently requires children to read and respond to non-fiction texts. So the programmes of study for KS1 mention:

> Pupils should be introduced to and should read information, both in print and on screen. They should be encouraged to make use of a range of sources of information, including dictionaries, IT-based reference materials, encyclopaedias and information presented in fictional form (*Range* p.6).

> Pupils should be taught to use reference materials for different purposes. They should be taught about the structural devices for organising information, eg *contents, headings,captions* (*Key Skills* p.8).

and later for KS2:

Pupils should read and use a wide range of sources of information, including those not specifically designed for children. The range of non-fiction should include IT-based reference materials, newspapers, encyclopaedias, dictionaries and thesauruses (*Range* p.13).

Pupils should be taught how to find information in books and computer-based sources by using organisational devices to help them decide which parts of the material to read closely. They should be given opportunities to read for different purposes, adopting appropriate strategies for the task, including skimming to gain an overall impression, scanning to locate information and detailed reading to obtain specific information. Pupils should be taught to:

- pose pertinent questions about a topic they are investigating
- identify the precise information that they wish to know
- distinguish between fact and opinion
- consider an argument critically
- make succinct notes
- use dictionaries, glossaries and thesauruses to explain unfamiliar vocabulary
- note the meaning and use of newly encountered words
- re-present information in different forms.

Pupils should be taught to use library classification systems, catalogues and indexes (*Key Skills* p.14).

Although under the NC children should be encountering non-fiction texts from the beginning of compulsory schooling, children's initial familiarity as readers is bound to be with fiction and the language structures which characterise narrative prose. In terms of reading style, this experience of narrative prose conditions young readers to process a text at a fairly uniform speed from beginning to end, sometimes called 'receptive' reading. This term does not do full justice to the demands of fiction reading where an active, reflective stance is often required by good quality writing. However, there is no doubt that the reading requirements of non-narrative texts are different.

The Schools Council project mentioned earlier, *The Effective Use of Reading*, directed by Eric Lunzer and Keith Gardner, looked at the ways in which teachers could develop different reading styles in their pupils. The researchers found that pupils tended to apply a continuous, one-paced, receptive style of reading to information texts right across the curriculum and simply gave up when the texts proved too difficult for this approach. Lunzer and Gardner suggested that teachers needed to guide pupils into a more flexible approach so that, in addition to a receptive style, they also had within their repertoire these additional styles, sometimes called 'higher order' reading skills:

- *reflective reading*: interrogating the text, setting up a 'conversation' with it

- *skimming*: picking up the gist of a text by the eye continuously and rapidly passing over it

- *scanning*: searching for relevant words and headings, the eye jumping around in the text

As the NC suggests, pupils ought then to be able to select the reading style most appropriate to the text and the purpose concerned (eg scanning a telephone directory, skimming an encyclopaedia to find a relevant passage and then reading it refectively).

The traditional means by which English teachers tried to stimulate these alternative styles of reading, the comprehension exercise, was not one which motivated readers or developed skills which pupils transferred to their subject or topic reading. These exercises also tended to be based more on literary than on information texts. As an alternative to decontextualised comprehension work, Lunzer and Gardner developed what they referred to as Directed Activities Related to Texts (DARTs). The texts in question might be either narrative or non-narrative. The main features of DARTs, treated in detail in Lunzer and Gardner's follow-up report *Learning from the Written Word* (1984), are:

- they are based on texts relevant to the subject or topic being studied

- they use group or pair discussion

- they present extracts from texts to pupils in two forms, either modified or unmodified

Modified Texts

In this kind of activity the texts which children are given to read are altered in one of these three main ways:

- deletion of words at intervals determined by the teacher (best suited to *expository* texts)

- altering the sequence of a passage by changing the order of words, lines, sentences or paragraphs (best suited to *instructional* texts)

- deleting a passage and requiring readers to predict what has happened or will happen (best suited to *narrative* texts)

For an example of a DART using a modified passage from an instructional text in order to stimulate reflective reading (see page 48).

It is essential first of all to get children to *cut up* the instructions before trying to re-order them. Group discussion is also indispensable in this 'reconstruction' activity and there is certainly scope for debate about the different possible orderings. As with all DARTs there is no right or wrong answer. Careful reading and reflection will be necessary to arrive at a satisfactory sequence.

For an example of a DART using deletion to 'direct' the group reading of an expository text on the topic of Change in Schools see page 49.

With completion activities such as this the length of passage and the number and type of words (phrases and sentences) deleted can be varied to suit teacher purpose and pupil ability. In this passage of exactly 200 words there are 13 deletions, a deliberately low ratio. The intention here is to direct attention to the significant words and concepts as a subject for discussion: so the deletions are of 'meaning' words, not random or in any particular frequency as in 'cloze procedure'. As a rule of thumb, deletions should not usually be more frequent than every seventh word and an introductory section of at least a few sentences should be left intact to create the context.

PUT THESE INSTRUCTIONS IN WHAT YOUR GROUP THINKS IS THE BEST ORDER. AT THE MOMENT THEY ARE JUMBLED UP:

HOW TO MAKE A WINDOW BOX

1. Fill with a mixture of rich soil and leaf-mould.

2. Trim the grass with scissors when it grows too long.

3. Paint the inside with a good wood preservative.

4. You will need a vegetable box, hand-drill, paint, wood-preservative and stones.

5. Choose a sunny window-sill and cut the box to fit its length.

6. Sow grass seeds in the centre or on one side.

7. Drill some holes in the bottom to allow any excess water to drain away.

8. Window-boxes can be made at home from an old vegetable box about 20 cm deep.

9. This will divide the box and you can grow clusters of flowers on each side.

10. Paint the box a bright colour.

11. Cover the bottom with small pieces of broken crockery or stones.

READ THIS PASSAGE IN YOUR GROUP AND THEN DECIDE BETWEEN YOU WHICH WORDS BEST FIT IN THE GAPS.

NEW WAYS OF TEACHING

'What do you think?'

If you were at school in 1900 you would probably never hear your teacher ask this question. Teachers had lists of what their pupils were supposed to know. Their job was to make sure that everyone learnt the same thing. In Art lessons everyone drew the same vase. In English lessons everyone read the same stories.

This was partly because many _____ did not know a great deal themselves. Some had just left _____ . They taught during the day and went to _____ classes in the evenings. There was very little _____ in schools so there was not much variety in the _____ .

All these things began to _____ slowly. After 1903 no-one was allowed to _____ until they reached the age of sixteen. In 1925 _____ who wanted to be teachers had to stay at school until they were eighteen and then go to _____ _____ for two years.

One of the most _____ changes came in a report written by the Department of Education in 1931. It said that teachers in _____ school should allow children to have their own _____ instead of always being told everything.

[Taken from: *Schools,* Judith Crosher (1989), p 20]

Unmodified Texts

Here the emphasis is on developing strategies which readers can use to extract relevant information from texts through what are sometimes called 'analysis' activities. Pupils might be required to compile a list, table or flow chart from data contained in a passage of expository or instructional writing. Alternatively they might be asked to draw or complete a map, diagram or picture. Additionally, labelling of paragraphs or underlining/ highlighting of key words, phrases and sentences might be required.

In all DARTs work, matching the demands of the reading task to the ability of the reader is another important consideration. The demands are varied, usually by decreasing the length or reading difficulty ('readability') of the passage; by using pictures as well as words; by reducing the number of deletions made in cloze procedure; and by increasing the number of clues (first letters of words, length of gap left, etc.) or the information supplied (data already filled in on a map or diagram).

Without careful matching of tasks to pupils and without genuine discussion, this type of reading development work can, of course, become simply a game or puzzle and one at which the best readers always come first. The danger needs to be guarded against if real reading for learning is to take place.

Work on ways of developing children's literacy through engagement with non-fiction texts has continued through recent reseach by, for example, Littlefair (1990), Neate (1992) and the Exeter Extending Literacy Project (EXEL) at the University of Exeter. Neate has coined the term 'structural guiders' to refer to the 'organisational devices' used in information books which young readers need to be able to recognise and use effectively, and which the 1995 AT2 specifically mentions (p.14). Examples of these are:

- the book cover
- index
- introduction/preface/foreword
- advance organisers (a passage introducing the main text)
- table of contents
- headings

- illustrations
- references to illustrations
- bibliography
- glossary
- summaries/reviews
  (Neate pp.62-72)

Littlefair has also focused teachers' attention on the distinctive and varied registers and genres of non-fiction texts, their differing conventions of style, vocabulary and organisation, which again children need guided opportunities to experience and recognise. The continuing EXEL Project has developed teaching strategies for reading and writing information texts based on a model of interaction, which is *not* intended as a linear description (Wray and Lewis, 1994) (see page 52).

Monitoring and assessment of reading

Pupils' Own Records

The 1989 programmes of study for Reading at KS2 required that pupils should 'keep records of their own reading and comment, in writing or in discussion, on the books which they have read' (p.31). This made a legal requirement of what had always been 'good practice' in the primary school. Keeping personal records of what they read gives pupils a sense of ownership of their reading and a responsibility for monitoring and reflecting on their own reading development. Pupils' own records, at a minimum, could be a simple list of titles and authors, with dates started and finished, and perhaps a 'star rating' of some kind, which could function as a bookmark. With older pupils a reading log in diary form will give scope for written comments where appropriate (not for *every* book). As well as the benefits for pupils, these self-maintained records make the class teacher's monitoring of reading activity much more manageable.

Teacher Assessment

In the National Curriculum 'Teacher Assessment' refers to the teacher's own records of children's achievements (not to the assessment of teachers!). In the particular area of reading, teachers will gather their own

Process Stages	Questions
1. Elicitation of previous knowledge.	1. What do I already know about this subject?
2. Establishing purposes.	2. What do I need to find out and what will I do with the information?
3. Locating information	3. Where and how will I get this information?
4. Adopting an appropriate strategy.	4. How should I use this source of information to get what I need?
5. Interacting with text.	5. What can I do to help me understand this better?
6. Monitoring understanding.	6. What can I do if there are parts I do not understand?
7. Making a record.	7. What should I make a note of from this information?
8. Evaluating information.	8. What items of information should I believe and which should I keep an open mind about?
9. Assisting memory.	9. How can I help myself remember the important parts?
10. Communicating information.	10. How should I let other people know about this?

information about pupil attainment most often through extended interviews with them, often known as 'reading conferences'.

The practice of holding individual consultations with pupils was strongly recommended by the *Extending Beginning Reading* project referred to earlier. This research pointed to the ineffectiveness of the traditional primary practice of children 'reading to teacher' for very short periods of time each day. The average time the teacher heard (perhaps with one ear) any one child read was found to be 30 seconds, too short for any effective teaching or help (Southgate et al, 1981 pp.320-1). Instead longer but less frequent individual contacts with children were suggested, reorganising the teacher's time so that, for example, 8 or 9 children could be seen every week for 15-20 minutes.

A planned programme of conferences will, of course, need to be worked out, with more frequent meetings with children who have reading difficulties and perhaps with some small group conferences for fluent readers. During the reading conference the child will usually read aloud from a self-chosen book for a few pages, then there will be discussion of the contents of the book, checking comprehension and sharing responses. Pupil-teacher discussion will also cover how and why the book was chosen and the child's past and future reading choices, making reference to the pupil's own records and planning ahead.

When the teacher listens to the child reading during a conference, she or he may also decide to take the opportunity to assess the child's performance for diagnostic and recording purposes. This assessment might take the form of either:

- an informal assessment
- a running record
- a simplified miscue analysis
- a full miscue analysis

These are more or less detailed methods of recording the errors children make as they read aloud. These mistakes are referred to as 'miscues', a term deriving from the work of Kenneth and Yetta Goodman (1973). Miscues can give an insight into how individual children read, indicating the 'cues' they are attending to or are failing to perceive as they process text. Analysis of miscues may reveal a pattern which can shed light on the reading strategies and approaches a child is using. Miscue analysis was recommended by the *Extended Beginning Reading* project as an important part of a reading conference programme.

Miscues can be divided into different types: substitutions, omissions and insertions. Analysis would also record pauses, repetitions, refusals and self-corrections. Of these, substitutions can often be the most revealing miscues and can be analysed further in a worthwhile way in relation to those four levels of written language referred to earlier. So substitutions can be either:

- similar in sound
- similar in shape
- syntactically similar
- or similar in sense

to the actual word on the page which the child has thus misread. For example, reading 'boat' for 'ship' would be a substitution which was similar in terms of syntax and sense, but quite dissimilar in terms of sound and shape. Analysis of miscues in this way can reveal over-attention to one or other level of language in reading strategies: in the above case, an over-reliance on meaning and contextual cues at the expense of grapho-phonic ones. Diagnosis of a pattern of similar miscues might suggest the need for phonics work on initial sounds or word recognition activities.

The *Primary Language Record* teacher's handbook devotes appendices to detailed descriptions of different miscue recording procedures.(pp. 58-63) The Informal Assessment described there consists of the teacher listening to a child reading aloud from a familiar book and observing and noting significant (but not all) miscues, as well as other features of reading listed on a reading record sheet. The procedure takes place, as do all forms of analysis of miscues, within the context of a normal classroom reading interview.

The Running Record takes this technique a stage further. Here the teacher has a copy of the text and, as the child reads aloud, the teacher marks up the particular passage to be analysed with a code of symbols which represent: words read correctly(/), substitutions (written above text), omissions (circled), words told by teacher (T) and self-corrections (SC). This marked passage then provides a sample which can be scrutinised for any significant pattern of miscueing and for assessment of reading strategies. The Running Record was used in the 1991-93 SATs for AT2 to confirm achievement at level 2 (SEAC, 1991a, 1993).

Simplified Miscue Analysis, as devised by Cliff Moon (1992), involves recording just two miscue types, substitutions and refusals (and also, incidentally, self-corrections). These are recorded in a table, as the child reads during a reading conference (see page 56).

The design of the table enables rapid but systematic analysis of substitutions against the four 'cueing systems' involved in reading. 'Negative' miscues, those which alter the meaning significantly, are distinguished here, as in the *Primary Language Record*, from 'positive' ones which suggest reading for meaning. The optional numerical analysis to work out a 'negative miscue rate' can give an approximate level of reading fluency helpful in choosing reading material.

Full miscue analysis usually involves the tape-recording of children's reading, then marking up of the text read with coding symbols and subsequent analysis of all types of miscue.(see Southgate et al pp.268-71 for an example). Although yielding the most detailed findings, miscue analysis in its original form is time-consuming and does introduce an element of artificiality at odds with normal classroom routines. Usually an unfamiliar text is used also. It would be impractical to use this procedure routinely in reading conferences therefore.

Guidance on teacher assessment of reading within the National Curriculum also recommends the use of the reading conference and some form of miscue analysis. The SEAC training materials for classroom assessment of English give a video-taped example of the reading conference for (SEAC, 1991c). The advice of the 1989 English Working Group on reading assessment stressed the need, as with oracy, for assessment to 'arise naturally out of good primary practice'. It recommended the format of the *Primary Language Record* as one on which teachers' record- keeping might be modelled. Such records would need to cover, as well as 'the child's reading strategies and approaches

DATE 16·3·90   NAME Gareth   CLASS 3   AGE 7   YEAR 2

TITLE & PAGE(S) OF BOOK The farmer and his sons

	SUBSTITUTIONS		Similarity			
	Word printed	Word read	Sound	Look	Part of speech	Meaning
1	GREW	GAVE	✓	✓	✓	✗
2	GREAT	GOLD	✓	✓	✓	✗
3	LET US	LET'S	✓	✓	✓	✓
4	DUG	DIGGED	✓	✓	✓	✓
5	WORKED	WALKED				
6	PENNY	PIECE	✓	✓	✓	✗
7	COULD	COULDN'T	✓	✓	✓	✗
8	SOON	SONS	✓	✓	✗	✗
9	GREW	GAVE	REPEAT—	DO NOT	COUNT	
10	MARKET	MONEY	✓	✓	✓	✗
11						
12						

Tally of refusals	⎯ ⫽⫽⫽⫽

Negative miscue rate   = $\dfrac{\text{Meaning (X) PLUS Refusals}}{\text{Total no. of words read}}$ × 100 = $\dfrac{11}{146}$ × 100

=   8   %

LEVEL   =   independent/instructional/frustration
                    (1%)   (5%)   ↑   (10%)

Notes on Miscue Analysis   Readability of book about right;
        Plenty of confidence , Think about meaning : CLOZE?

when handling a familiar text', as revealed by analysis of miscues, the following information:

- what the child has read
- levels of comprehension
- retrieval of information
- the child's reading tastes and preferences
  (Cox, 1989 paras. 16.46-16.50)

The 1995 NC provides Level Descriptions which lay down criteria against which children's reading development can be considered for reporting purposes. These are, as with AT1, holistic profiles of developing readers but may be analysed into three main strands:

- initial reading
- range of and response to reading
- information retrieval

Progression is defined in these strands as below:

AT2 READING: LEVEL DESCRIPTIONS

Initial Reading

level 1: Pupils recognise familiar words in simple texts. They use their knowledge of letters and sound-symbol relationships in order to read words and to establish meaning when reading aloud. In these activities they sometimes require support.

level 2: Pupils' reading of simple texts shows understanding and is generally accurate. They use more than one strategy, such as phonic, graphic, syntactic and contextual, in reading unfamiliar words and establishing meaning.

level 3: Pupils read a range of texts fluently and accurately. They read independently, using strategies appropriately to establish meaning.

Range and Response

level 1: They express their response to poems, stories and non- fiction by identifying aspects they like.

level 2: They express opinions about major events or ideas in stories, poems and non-fiction.

level 3: In responding to fiction and non-fiction they show understanding of the main points and express preferences.

level 4: In responding to a range of texts, pupils show understanding of significant ideas, themes, events and characters, beginning to use inference and deduction. They refer to the text when explaining their views.

level 5: Pupils show understanding of a range of texts, selecting essential points and using inference and deduction where appropriate, In their responses, they identify key features, themes and characters, and select sentences, phrases and relevant information to support their views.

level 6: In reading and discussing a range of texts, pupils identify different layers of meaning and comment on their significance and effect. They give personal responses to literary texts, referring to aspects of language, structure and themes in justifying their views.

Information Retrieval

level 3: They use their knowledge of the alphabet to locate books and find information.

level 4: They locate and use ideas and information.

level 5: They retrieve and collate information from a range of sources.

level 6: They summarise a range of information from different sources.

It seems appropriate to end with some advice given by SEAC on the importance of *all* reading assessments, including SATs, being seen as part of normal classroom routines and as relevant to what is going on in the classroom: 'reading assessment should be as relaxed and enjoyable as your normal experience of sharing a book with a child' (SEAC, 1993 p.7).

Further Reading

Benton, M. and Fox, G. (1985) *Teaching Literature 9-14.* Oxford: Oxford University Press.

Cairney, T. (1990) *Teaching Reading Comprehension.* Buckingham: Open University Press.

Gawith, G. (1990) *Reading Alive !* London: A&C Black.

Mallett, M. (1992) *Making Facts Matter.* London: Paul Chapman Publishing.

Moon, C. and Raban, B. (1992) *A Question of Reading.* London: David Fulton.

Neate, B. (1992) *Finding Out About Finding Out.* London: Hodder and Stoughton.

Chapter Three

WRITING

The Background

Only comparatively recently has writing, the second R, received the same kind of attention as reading from educationists and researchers. The Newbolt report endorsed the view that 'composition' was 'the most valuable exercise in the school', closely linked to 'the growth of the mind' and the development of individuality (p.72) but devoted only one small section to it and far more space to 'literature'.

More recent debate about writing in the English curriculum has focused on the relative importance of the individual and social dimensions of the activity. Is the aim primarily personal growth or adult needs? The increasing use of 'creative writing' approaches (sometimes called 'personal' or 'intensive' writing) in primary schools in thc latc 1950s and 60s challenged traditional practice which used composition and exercises to develop pupils' writing. The new approach, which never completely supplanted the traditional methods, valued qualities of spontaneity and originality above those of composing within a framework of prescribed form and content. Imaginative expression was seen as possible, even preferable, before practice in acquiring writing techniques. Attention was therefore paid to stimulating the writer and to exploiting first hand experiences: 'the excitement of writing' was what was important (Clegg, 1964).

Research into classroom writing in the 1970s by influential figures such as James Britton concentrated on 'the development of writing abilities' (Britton et al, 1975). This was concerned with how children's written language developed over the years of secondary education and also with attempts to classify types of writing by function. So Britton and his team divided writing into the 'expressive', which is personal and uses language 'close to the speaker'; the 'transactional', which uses language more impersonally and explicitly in order to achieve an end; and the 'poetic', where language is used 'for its own sake, and not as a means of achieving something else' (p.91). In developmental terms, expressive writing was seen as fundamental: children moved along a continuum from this to poetic writing (for example, stories, plays and poems) in the 'role of the spectator', as a detached observer, and along another continuum to transactional writing (reports, arguments, instructions) in the 'role of the participant', involved in the business of getting something done.

The work of Britton and his team emphasised function and audience in children's writing. Influential publications in the 1980s by researchers such as Frank Smith (1982) and Donald Graves (1983) put the stress on the processes involved in writing and the need to make children aware of these (Newbolt (p.74) had mentioned the lack of this sixty years earlier). Smith made a basic division of the writing process into composition (authorial) and transcription (secretarial) aspects. Graves was influential in promoting an apprenticeship approach to writing which gave children the opportunity to choose the topics they wanted to write about, to write for as long as they needed, to draft and revise their work, to discuss it with other children and with their teacher during 'conferences' or extended interviews and to 'publish' the writing in some form within the classroom or school. The processes the young writer was encouraged to go through were, it was argued, those which any adult author and secretary would use: getting ideas, drafting, re-writing, getting responses, editing, proof-reading and publishing. The child as individual author was still at the centre of the writing curriculum, as in the creative writing approach, but a concern with the crafting of writing within a workshop setting had replaced unrehearsed spontaneity.

Most recently in the late 1980s and 1990s the ascendancy of the process-based teaching of writing has been challenged by researchers who have sought to re-emphasise the social rather than the personal context of writing. Pam Gilbert, for example, has questioned the 'romantic' notion of children as authors and the 'privileging' of the writing of certain forms of literary or expressive texts, particularly the story (Gilbert,1990, p.62). She sees Graves' approach to writing as directly descended from the personal growth school established as orthodoxy in the 1960s. Emphasis on the mystique of authorship, Gilbert argues, actually confuses and disadvantages young writers (p.77) rather than empowering them.

In place of 'writing conceived of as natural — as personal, original creativity', Gilbert puts forward a concept of writing as 'social, textual construction' (p.63). Thus: 'Learning how to write an effective short story or a modern lyric can be compared with learning how to participate in a formal debate, or learning how to chair a meeting' (p.76). This is often described as a 'genre-based' approach to writing which stresses that there are teachable and learnable rules relating to different types of writing, non-fiction as well as fiction. A corollary of this is that children should learn to write in, as well as to read, many different genres or forms not only the privileged literary ones. There is a renewed interest here in the social dimension of written language, but as part of a cultural analysis view of English rather than an adult needs or cultural heritage view.

The 1985-89 National Writing Project (NWP), an extensive investigation and curriculum development exercise, has been an important influence in mediating writing research for the classroom. The project's work has highlighted the importance of audience and purpose in children's writing; the need for children to appreciate and engage with the processes involved in writing; but also the collaborative nature of writing activities and the need to experience a range of forms.

The NWP's influence on the 1989 and 1995 curricula has been substantial. In both programmes of study there are clear references to children developing the ability to use the processes of writing:

> Pupils should be given opportunities to plan, draft and improve their work on paper and on screen, and to discuss and evaluate their own and others' writing. To develop their writing, pupils should be taught to:

- *plan* — note and develop initial ideas
- *draft* — develop ideas from the plan into structured written text
- *revise* — alter and improve the draft
- *proofread* — check the draft for spelling and punctuation errors, omissions or repetitions
- *present* — prepare a neat, correct and clear final copy

Pupils should be encouraged to develop their ability to organise and structure their writing in a variety of ways, using their experience of fiction, poetry and other texts. (1995 p.15)

In addition, the importance of writing in different social and cultural contexts is emphasised: 'Pupils should be taught to identify the purpose for which they write and to write for a range of readers...' (p.9). The programmes of study also specify that pupils should experience a variety of writing activities: 'Pupils should be taught to organise and present their writing in different ways, helpful to the purpose, task and reader. They should be taught to write in a range of forms, incorporating some of the different characteristics of those forms' (p.9).

The 1989 curriculum followed Smith (1982) in distinguishing 'composing' and 'transcribing' aspects of the writing process, and in insisting that 'the secretarial aspect should not be allowed to predominate in the assessment' (Cox, 1991 p.140). The design of the writing profile component mirrored this: AT3 was concerned with composing, including punctuation and grammatical structure, whereas spelling and handwriting were dealt with in separate ATs, 4 and 5.

The 1995 curriculum abolishes this division between composing and transcribing dimensions. Instead of three ATs there is only one which covers:

- compositional skills (including grammatical structure)
- presentational skills (punctuation, spelling and handwriting)
- use of a widening variety of forms for different purposes (p.2)

There is a greater emphasis on grammatical features, in the teaching and assessment of pupils' 'compositional skills', although the programmes of study also stress writing as 'a source of enjoyment' and 'enjoyable in itself' and the Level Descriptions also refer explicitly to qualities of writing such as 'interest and liveliness' which the Cox curriculum reluctantly decided were not possible to assess (Cox, 1991 p.147). Presentational features are part of the assessment of writing at every level, but as elements within a holistic description of writing development, they should not 'predominate in the assessment' as Cox warned.

Writing Development

In both the 1989 and 1995 AT3s, writing development is defined in terms of a growing ability to construct and convey meaning. The 1989 levels of attainment designed to measure this growth began with this first stage: 'Pupils should be able to: use pictures, symbols or isolated letters, words or phrases to communicate meaning' (1989 p.12). This is echoed in the 1995 programmes of study: 'Pupils' early experiments and independent attempts at communicating in writing, using letters and known words, should be encouraged' (1995 p.9), even though assessment of writing now begins further on in the developmental cycle in the first Level Description. The key is the attempt to create and convey meaning through mark-making. Even before what we conventionally call 'writing' is learnt, this first crucial step has to be taken. It will of course have to take place in the meaningful context of interaction in the home or the nursery/infant classroom and also in the context of spoken language competence and reading experiences.

The phenomenon of 'emergent literacy' (Hall, 1987) has been increasingly studied and valued. Research has placed greater importance than previously on children's first attempts at scribbling and mark-making. These and other early scripting activities are seen as the beginnings of literate behaviour themselves, not indicators of a kind of 'writing-readiness' but indications that writing development has already begun. The emphasis on this approach to children's early writing behaviour is on what the writers *can* do rather than what they can't.

'This is writing' (Amy, aged 2½)

Writing, like reading, is a complex activity in which a number of discrete processes and skills are 'orchestrated' simultaneously (Newman, 1984). To write involves:

- having something to communicate

- making appropriate language choices

- co-ordinating fine motor skills

- organising what we want to say

- using necessary secretarial skills.

The transition from spoken to written language will require the child to use a significantly different mode of communication. When we write rather than speak we face these new challenges (Perera, 1984):

- no immediate feedback

- no immediate context

- no use of intonation or stress

- more structural rules

- a fixed, not a transient form

- a much slower production of meaning

The beginner writer has to learn how to convey meaning to an audience now distant in time, place and situation.

Initially writing will grow out of oral language and reflect its patterns and organisation. Writing will lag behind a child's spoken language competence for some time. Kroll (1981) has suggested the following relationships between speaking and writing at different phases of children's development:

- a preparation phase
- a consolidation phase
- a differentiation phase
- an integration phase

In the preparation phase the basic skills of handwriting and orthography are being mastered: whilst this phase is under way the sheer physical effort of transcribing constrains written communication so that children are able to say far more than they can write. The consolidation phase is reached when children can put down on the page what they are already able to express through speech. Writing at this stage will have many of the characteristics of speech. At the differentiation stage the motor skills involved in the physical act of writing have become semi-automatic and the young writer is able to focus on vocabulary, stylistic and organisational choices. Writing then differentiates itself from speech, having 'caught up' with it, and the distinctive features of literary language begin to appear. The process is two-way and the influence of written language can be heard in speech also. Kroll's final integrated stage involves a re-discovery of personal voice and 'naturalness' in writing, an advanced phase which not all writers will reach.

Although it is not possible or desirable to attach specific age-limits to Kroll's phases, Perera (1984) tentatively suggests about 6 or 7 for the onset of the consolidation phase and 9 or 10 for the differentiation phase, basing her figures on large-scale surveys of children's writing.

It is important to see the relationship between spoken and written language as one of cross-fertilisation at all phases. It would be as naive to see the development of writing as the ability to write down speech as it would be to suggest speech should begin to sound like writing once a child is literate. From the beginning oral language experiences will need to inform and underpin children's explorations into writing. Once the differences inherent in the written mode have been realised and exploited, the challenge will then be to convey some of the vitality and interest of speech on the page.

Writing in the Classroom: Processes

A Y1 class is grouped together on a carpeted area in front of the teacher, who has a large sheet of paper pinned to the wall beside her. The class have been discussing what they might write about and decided it will be a story about a favourite toy which gets lost. They are now collaborating to write this story with the teacher acting as class scribe. Contributions and ideas are encouraged from everyone and alternatives considered before the writing proceeds. The teacher prompts the class with questions and suggestions. As she scribes, she comments on the features of written language being used, such as the left to right directionality and the spaces between words. The story will not be finished in this session since the teacher will stop when she feels the children have done enough. Tomorrow they will look back at what they have written so far and either go on with it or begin a new story.

This kind of shared writing where the adult acts as secretary for children at the consolidation phase in their writing development is a familiar strategy in the KS1 classroom, providing a bridge to literacy. Oral language is exploited to the full as a resource for planning, rehearsing and reviewing writing. These children are able to see their teacher act out the kind of choices and decisions that have to be made in order to make the transition from speech to writing. As she prompts them she models the kind of inner dialogue experienced writers learn to use. The 1995 NC requires just this kind of teacher support: 'Teachers should, on occasions, help pupils to compose at greater length by writing for them, demonstrating the way that ideas may be recorded in print' (p.9). Later in their infant experience these children will be involved in whole class oral discussion of, and rehearsals for, writing which they will then undertake themselves in groups, pairs or individually, frequently with the teacher or other adult acting as scribe. As they move towards becoming independent writers, planning and rehearsing their writing in pairs or groups, the children will continue to use the processes that have been modelled for them from the very beginning.

Recognising that children learn to write by reading and vice versa, the teacher also frequently shares 'big books' with the class in a similar way. These are large-scale replicas of commercially available children's books which allow the text and pictures to be easily seen by all the children during a whole class reading. As Moon (1994) comments: 'Using 'big books' with younger children clearly demonstrates how the reader processes text to unlock meanings and stories *and* models written language forms and conventions.'

The classroom itself is also full of examples of writing used for different purposes and in a variety of writing styles: capitals,printing, cursive. An alphabet frieze is on display for reference. There are notices and labels, captions for wall displays, a board featuring words found on packets and wrappers, and a message board at the right height for the children to use, encouraging dialogue between the children themselves and with adults. Children's own writing is displayed on other boards. An attractive writing area has been established where a variety of pencils, papers and envelopes are freely available for use. In another area, a newsagent's shop has been set up to provide a meaningful setting for literacy activities. Here are many examples of different types of written texts: books, magazines, comics, national and local newspapers, puzzle books, greetings cards, postcards, some of which have been made by the children themselves. There are also posters, labels, lists and adverts around the shop which need to be renewed frequently.

In this environment children in the initial stages of writing development are being encouraged to 'become writers rather than merely learning to write' (Tann, 1991 p.222). Learning to write, in fact, is seen as going beyond the traditional tracing or copying of handwriting, usually to produce captions for pictures, often found at this stage. Support with transcription constraints means that young writers are able to orchestrate *all* the processes involved in writing from the start, rather than moving step-by-step up a ladder of separate writing skills.

This classroom approach to writing which emphasises discussion, collaboration and modelling by the teacher of the processes of authorship continues at KS2. Here, a more structured form of workshop organisation will be appropriate, for children entering the consolidation and later the differentiation phases in their development as writers, increasing in experience, independence and confidence. Let's look at an example of this organisation in practice:

A Y5 class is involved in a writing workshop session, one of two which take place each week for an hour at a time. At the moment the children are writing silently. This is an essential part of each session when everyone is engaged in a kind of Uninterrupted Sustained Silent Writing, including the teacher. At the end of this fifteen-minute period the activity in the classroom will become more diverse. Some children will discuss their work with a 'response partner', a specific person with whom they will regularly talk about each other's writing. Other writers will have a 5 or 10 minute 'conference' with the teacher, alone or in a small group, to review their work so far. The topics the Y5 children are writing about are their own choices but assisted by previous demonstrations of topic-choice by the teacher and by discussions with their partners. The development from using of collaborative talk to generate and sustain writing in the KS1 classroom is clear.

As a result of their consultations and the responses received some children are working on re-drafting their writing. This particular process has again been modelled and talked about with the whole class. The principle of drafting is firmly established and the difference between revising (reworking text for the writer's sake) and editing (reworking for the reader's sake) is understood (Smith, 1982 p.127). Other writers *are* at the editing stage, where they will rely firstly on their own resources and then their partner's, before going to the teacher as editor-in-chief for a final proof-reading check. Those who have been through this stage are making a final copy of their writing, some using a word-processing program, or making the finished copy into a simple book form for publication. This might mean display within the classroom, loan to other classes, or the book being placed in a section of the school library.

A display board in the classroom draws children's attention to the processes they are working through in their workshop writing and the order in which they should undertake them. A flow chart traces the journey of a piece of writing through the stages of Getting Ideas, Planning, Drafting, Revising, Editing and Publishing. Also on this board is a rota of conferences arranged with the teacher, for which the children can sign up and on the table in front of it are the boxes where writing folders are stored between sessions, as well as other materials, such as paper, binding materials, dictionaries, thesauruses, which might be useful (see Gregory et al, 1990).

The teacher is conscious that the writing-workshop procedures must not become set in concrete: any form of inflexible orthodoxy will defeat its own purposes in the end. So not all the classroom writing the children undertake in a week is within the workshop format. Sometimes during workshops the organisation is varied by, for example:

- the teacher suggesting a particular genre or topic for the writing

- the teacher giving a short introduction to explore the suggested form or content of the writing

- the teacher focusing for part of the workshop on an aspect of children's writing (style, organisation, spelling, grammar, punctuation) with some or all of the class

Whatever adaptations are made in response to changing pupil needs, the teacher adheres to the principle that these young writers develop best by being given the time, motivation and support to engage with all the processes involved in authorship in a classroom where writing is valued and shared. However the organisation is varied, each session will end if possible with a sharing period of 5 or 10 minutes when children (and teacher) can read aloud some of their writing.

Writing in the Classroom: Audiences and Purposes

Rather than trying to provide physical stimuli to give children's writing a 'real' context, primary teachers have concentrated more recently on providing authentic audiences and purposes for classroom writing. Creating real audiences means attempting to go beyond the normal readership of children's writing — the child and the teacher — and beyond the usual purpose — to demonstrate competence to the teacher in skills, knowledge or understanding. It is an approach which can easily be accommodated within the process-based writing-workshop or can take place outside it.

Let's again look at two examples in the classroom:

A Y2 class are involved in writing a school guide book. Their audience is specific — next year's Reception children — and the purpose clear — to help the younger children settle into their new school by *informing* them about it. The children are able to draw on their own experiences, their memories of starting infant school and their current feelings about moving up to the junior school. They have also interviewed present R/Y1 children to find out what things surprised them in their new school. They have talked about the kind of information which should go in a guide and the best way to present it to younger children so it will also *entertain* them. A picture book will eventually be produced which will be distributed to the new intake. In it the words and thoughts of the Y2 children and their drawings and diagrams will be used throughout, including examples of each child's work. The teacher will take responsibility for the editorial task of producing the finished booklets.

A Y4 class are working in small groups to produce posters, pamphlets and an information pack relating to a local nature reserve they have recently visited. The materials are aimed at children of similar age in the locality, the posters and pamphlets to persuade them to visit the reserve, and the information pack to inform them about what can be seen there. The pack will consist of maps, drawings, descriptions of wildlife, interactive worksheets and a cassette tape which can be used when walking around the reserve. The posters and pamphlets will advertise the materials at the local library and tourist information office and they will be made available to other school parties when they visit the site. The finished materials will be desk-top published by another member of the school staff.

According to the 1995 NC: 'Pupils should be given opportunities to write for an extended range of readers, eg *the teacher, the class, other children, adults in the school or community, imagined audiences.'* (p.15). Children will certainly often be writing for themselves, their classmates and their teacher, but in addition to these immediate readerships a wider range of audiences is possible as in the two examples above. Audiences for children's writing can usually be determined by these variables:

- younger or older?
- child or adult?
- known or unknown?

So other examples of writing for different audiences might be:

- *For Older Known Adults*: producing a newsletter about the school community to distribute to old people in a nearby residential home the children often visit
- *For Older Unknown Children*: designing a questionnaire about reading and viewing habits and writing a report on the survey findings for secondary school pupils

As far as purposes of writing are concerned, these will always be intimately linked to the chosen audiences. Sometimes purposes will be decided on first, sometimes audiences, occasionally the two will be suggested simultaneously. Purposes will have an immediate aspect and an underlying one, as in the school guide for Reception children above. The immediate purpose should be the motivation behind the writing — to tell the new children about their school — and this needs to be uppermost in the mind from the outset. The underlying purposes will probably need to be made explicit at some point to more experienced writers. These might include the following:

- to entertain
- to inform
- to persuade
- to instruct
- to evaluate

Children can be made aware of how these fundamental purposes go beyond the immediate context of a piece of writing and can underlie a variety of different kinds of writing, for example reports, guide-books and encyclopaedias all seek to inform. They can also be shown that writing often combines two or more of these underlying purposes — so a guide-book might try to persuade and inform, a book review would evaluate and inform and so on.

Assessment of children's writing produced for specific reasons and readerships will need to incorporate feedback about appropriateness for audience and purpose. Involving wider audiences means involving them in responding to the children's work. So the Reception children's reactions to the school guide books, other visitors' comments on the information pack; all will have to be fed back to the authors. Teachers' comments on, and assessment of, the work will need to take account of these.

Writing in the Classroom: Forms

As well as ensuring that pupils write for a range of audiences and purposes, teachers will also want to ensure that 'a widening variety of forms' is experienced. (The term 'genre' is also often used to refer to the different types of writing we use conventionally: letters, reports, poems, plays etc.) Form is also closely bound up with audience and purpose and may be implied in the choices made there. Sometimes, however, a particular form of writing may suggest itself first to the teacher as one that she or he would like the children to experience. Audience and purpose might then be suggested and the writing proceed possibly in the workshop style described. For example, the teacher may decide that more experience of letter-writing is needed. She or he may then devise a context for the letters, which might be letters of praise or complaint (to a toy manufacturer, TV company or bookshop, for example) or personal letters (to a class in another school). The emphasis on a particular form would mean that discussion of features and techniques peculiar to that kind of written format would be prominent.

It should never be assumed that children will be aware of genre characteristics and able to use them appropriately in their writing. Producing travel agents' brochures, newspaper articles (for tabloid or broadsheet papers) or advertising copy, will require focusing on some of the formal characteristics of those kinds of writing, through reading examples and discussing the main features observed (how to describe places persuasively but still honestly; how to structure the main points of a newspaper story; how to create a unique selling point.)

The EXEL project mentioned in the context of reading non-fiction in Chapter Two has also generated effective teaching strategies in this area, in particular the use of 'writing frames'. These consist of a skeleton outline of key words and phrases, a kind of template which gives children a structure appropriate to a particular generic form within which they can communicate what they have to say. The EXEL team follow Christie (1989) in identifying six types of non-fiction: recount, report,explanation, discussion, exposition or persuasion and procedure. An example of an 'explanation frame', completed by a Y4 child, is given in Lewis and Wray's *Writing Frames* (see page 76).

It is stressed that the writing frames are intended to be used as 'scaffolding' and to be used at a particular phase in children's non-fiction writing. The teaching model used is again one which will begin with teacher modelling and demonstration, move into a phase of joint activity and then reach a stage of 'scaffolded' activity where the writing frames can be used to allow children to write in a supported way but without an adult alongside them. Once familiar with a form, writers should be able to 'outgrow' the frame, adapt and extend it and then move away from it to write independently in that genre. Writing frames thus support learners in the transition to writing non-fiction independently, avoiding the situation where children are asked to make the jump suddenly and unaided.

Discussion of generic features and experimentation with formal structures will be just as important for the development of forms of writing which we often assume 'everybody knows': story and poem. Children clearly listen to and read many examples of these in their early years and pick up some of the more obvious characteristics — that stories often begin 'One day...' or 'Once upon a time...' and end 'And then we went to bed' or 'They all lived happily ever after...'. Equally, full rhymes and pronounced rhythm are intuitively picked up as characteristics of poetry. To extend story and poem writing further, however, requires more structured intervention and support.

Samuel

I want to explain why The Tudors and Stuarts usually Used rivers instead of roads.

There are several reasons for this. The chief reason is That the roads were bad so the wheels would break and it would take ages to get ther.

Another reason is ther were robbers and thieves would Stele the horse.

A further reason is, The weather wald not afecad the River but it wauld, afered the road

So now you can see why The Tuodors used Rivers more then the bumppy old and a net roads!

Writing Stories

Help will be needed with narrative structure when children move from telling stories, at which most are adept, to writing stories. This can begin whilst children are at Kroll's preparation phase of writing development. Awareness of narrative form can be stimulated by reading, telling and talking about stories and by letting children tape-record stories themselves. Simple picture stories can be created to allow young children to experiment with narrative structure. A cartoon story, in 3 or 4 frames to begin with, can be cut up and given to pairs or groups to reassemble. How do changes in the ordering of the frames affect the story? Which order tells the story best? From here, a next step might be to add captions to the re-ordered frames.

As children progress from dependence on the teacher as scribe towards becoming independent writers, picture strips can help them at the planning stage of story-writing. This would involve writers individually or collaboratively filling in a basic storyboard to plot out the development of their narrative from beginning through middle to end. Writing could be in the form of captions or on a separate piece of paper:

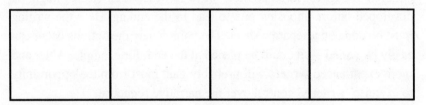

The National Writing Project (1987) developed various other useful formats for picture planning, such as the 'ladder':

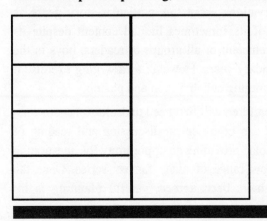

Here a sequence of four pictures can be drawn vertically down the left hand side of the page and the story then written in the right-hand space. This arrangement allows children to move from captioning storyboard pictures to producing continuous text where the writing runs in parallel to the visual plan. There is flexibility as well as a planning structure for the writer to follow.

Use of this type of planning aid can be extended to more elaborate formats, such as 'cross junctions' (NWP, 1987):

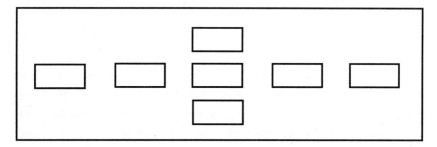

The 'cross junction' in the middle of the linear sequence encourages children to suggest three possible ways in which their stories might be developed before choosing one to lead to the ending. Here the writing must be done on a separate sheet. The point where the options occur can easily be varied — it could be placed at the end, for example. Abler and more experienced writers will probably gain most from the opportunity to exercise 'writerly' control over the narrative sequence.

Experience of story planning can be extended for older primary children by introducing the writing of 'Choose Your Own Adventure' books. Teachers often have reservations about this particular story genre as reading material because of its sometimes limited content despite its popularity with the most reluctant of all groups of readers, boys in the upper primary/lower secondary years. However as a writing exercise it has many benefits in encouraging collaboration and planning.

Working in small groups, children will first need to decide on characters, setting and scenario. This can be based on discussion and reading of examples of Adventure books, providing an opportunity for questioning the stereotyping and narrow range of many fantasy series. Once the parameters of the story have been agreed, careful planning is indispensable and story planners like the following will be needed to plot out the various story options the reader can follow:

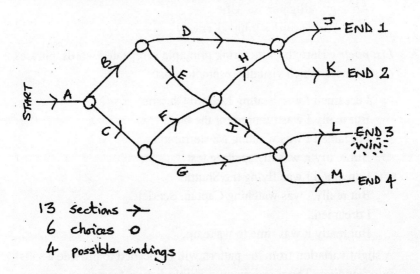

13 sections →
6 choices ○
4 possible endings

Following this design the adventure book would have an introductory passage, 13 sections (A-M) of continuous writing, 6 points where choices had to be made (indicated by the circles) and 4 possible endings. Simpler or more elaborate designs are obviously possible, but it is wise not to over-elaborate initially, as children often wish to do, adding complicated point-scoring systems.

A natural audience exists for the completed books amongst peers in the school and classroom: the purpose of challenge and entertainment is clear too, as is the problem-solving challenge of writing according to the formal (not necessarily stylistic) conventions of a distinctive contemporary genre.

Writing Poems

Development in poetry writing will involve children being offered structures of increasing sophistication to use as a kind of scaffolding for their own imaginations. Alternatives to rhyming organisation will have to be provided early on, but *always* using acrostics, for example, will be just as limiting. Children can use and return to all forms of poetry at all stages, but a planned progression might roughly follow a sequence like this:

- *Alliterative poetry.* Alphabet or counting poems can be constructed collaboratively:

  > An angry alligator ate Alfie
  > Two terrible turtles trapped Tracey

- *List poetry.* Here the structuring principle is repeated words, phrases or sentences which visually resemble a list:

  > I dreamed I was beating Linford Christie
  > But really I was running for the bus.
  > I dreamed I was winning Mastermind
  > But really it was my spelling test.
  > I dreamed I was flying the Shuttle
  > But really I was watching Captain Scarlett.
  > I dreamed...
  > But really it was time to wake up!

A slight variation from the pattern will be needed to provide a satisfying ending. There are many possible listing formats to use (see Corbett and Moses, 1986 pp.57-58)

- *Acrostic poetry.* These poems should spell out what they are about, usually down the left-hand side:

  > **E**njoyable always,
  > **N**ever dull,
  > **G**ood for the mind.
  > **L**anguage games,
  > **I**nteresting drama,
  > **S**torytelling,
  > **H**aiku too.
  >
  > **H**umid, sticky,
  > **E**very surface hot.
  > **A**ny change?
  > **T**emperature's rising!
  > **W**hen will it end?
  > **A**sphalt is melting,
  > **V**ery shortly
  > **E**verything else will too!

The individual lines of an acrostic can be one or more words and can be independent or run on continuously into the next. The important thing, which children sometimes lose sight of, is to focus on describing the thing spelled out.

- *Shape poetry*. Sometimes called concrete poems, these are actually more difficult to produce successfully than is usually imagined. As with acrostics, it is important to realise that the poem will make its meaning visually as well as verbally. Simply writing within a cut-out shape or round an outline can help young children focus on a subject, but fully realised shape poetry will go beyond this in the interconnection it makes between word and image:

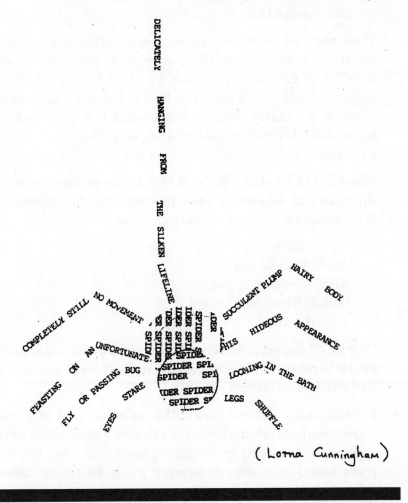

(Lorna Cunningham)

- *Syllabic poetry.* This time structure is provided by the number of syllables in the words used in each line and in the whole poem. This means children will need to be given examples of what a syllable is — a speech-sound containing a vowel pronounced as a unit within a word (poetry = po — et — ry, 3 syllables). The two best known syllabic forms have been imported into English poetry from Japanese: the tanka (5 lines of 31 syllables, 5,7,5,7,7) and the haiku (3 lines of 17 syllables, arranged 5,7,5):

  > AUTUMN HAIKU
  > Orange ochre leaf
  > Bats against our wet windscreen
  > Like a broken kite.

These restricted forms also require careful crafting if the simple structure is to be exploited fully. It is helpful to retain some of the discipline of the Japanese tradition where the haiku is strictly a snapshot of a significant moment, a frozen image not a narrative or argument, and usually about the natural world. If this focus is lost, haikus easily become limp and flabby despite the telegram-like word restriction.

Cinquains (5 lines of 22 syllables, 2,4,6,8,2) were the invention of an American poet, Adelaide Crapsey. They allow for more rhythmical development and can have a visual pattern too:

> Heron
> Hunched against rain,
> Skinny schoolboy in goal.
> Till neck telescopes erect and
> He strikes.

Once the syllabic principle and the use of restricted formats is grasped there is no reason why experienced writers should not go on to create their own syllable patterns.

- *Rhyming and/or metrical poetry.* This traditional form of poetic organisation is the one children become familiar with from their early experiences of listening to and reading poems. As a structure for poetry *writing* it is worth introducing, or re-introducing, later rather than sooner, to avoid poetry becoming associated purely with a search for rhyming words. To exploit more of the potential of rhyming poetry older writers can be introduced to half-rhymes (beanz meanz Heinz) as well as full rhymes; to rhyme which occurs in the middle as well as the end of lines.

Riddles are an effective way into creating poems which use rhyme and regular rhythm for a purpose, as in this example from Brian Patten's *Gargling with Jelly* (1985):

What Am I?
I go to where I came from,
I'm always passing and I stay,
Though I never move an inch
I go many miles each day.
(Answer: a road)

The limerick is usually the most successful format for comic rhyme and metre.

* *Free verse.* By definition this type of poetry is 'free' of all the above limits and restrictions. In practice successful free verse can exploit elements of any of them. It also relies on other patterns of organisation: the use of varied line lengths and line breaks and the incorporation of speech rhythms, for example. Michael Rosen, the most influential children's poet of the past twenty years, has shown how free verse can be used to help children write in their own language about their own experiences, drawing on anecdotes and authentic speech (Rosen, 1989). Rosen's own poetry, at its best, has an art which conceals art, subtly merging the repetitive patterning of poetry with the artless patter of talk, as in this example from *You Tell Me* (1979):

Rodge said,
'Teachers — they want it all ways —
You're jumping up and down on a chair
or something
and they grab hold of you and say,
"Would you do that sort of thing in your own home?"

'So you say, 'No.'
And they say,
'Well don't do it here then.'

'But if you say, 'Yes, I do it at home.'
they say,
'Well, we don't want that sort of thing
going on here thank you very much.'
'Teachers — they get you all ways,'
Rodge said.

Used like this, free verse can be enabling to the youngest poets. But its potential can also be exploited more fully by writers who have experienced a wide range of poetry structures, such as the ones above and many others, which is why I have left it until last.

The kind of poetry-writing progression sketched here will be most effective within a workshop approach where drafting, revising and editing processes can be used, when appropriate, for even the shortest poem. Relevant audiences and purposes can be offered too. The writing techniques involved should be used in an enabling, not a restrictive way and always capable of extension for abler writers. They can certainly be introduced through games and other activities as Sandy Brownjohn has demonstrated (Brownjohn, 1994). A repertoire of varied poetry structures should liberate children in the end to write about their own concerns:

> The most original writing has been produced when the children have been free to draw on their personal experiences but have been given a fairly clear structure within which to express themselves.
> (Gareth Davies, 1988, p.87)

Writing Across the Curriculum

If opportunities are to be found for children to write in a variety of forms, not only literary ones, and for a range of audiences and purposes, writing will need to be seen as taking place in every part of the primary curriculum. The core and foundation subjects of the NC offer many meaningful contexts for writing and many which extend children's writing experience into the non-chronological, non-narrative forms they encounter less frequently as writers. Examples of such contexts might be:

- *Maths*: As part of their work on data-handling, Y3 pupils produce bar charts and pictographs representing children's breakfast cereal preferences. Results are presented in a report drawn up as consultants to a major manufacturer

- *Science*: Y4 pupils investigate the colour properties of a number of brands of felt-tipped pens and compile as a class a *Which*-style comparative survey of their findings

- *Geography*: A Y6 class write and record in small groups a short video sequence, for infant viewers, to explain the water cycle

- *P.E.*: Y3/4 pupils devise their own games for field or playground and draw up rules and then possible tactics for playing them

- *Design and Technology*: A Y2 class generate ideas for, design, make and then evaluate card games for children of their own age

As well as writing being used as a means of presenting and reporting in different subjects and topics like these, it also needs to be seen as a tool for learning, to be used before and during, not only at the end of projects. Children might use 'writing for learning' in this way, to:

- frame questions for research
- take notes from books
- construct questionnaires
- plan interviewing
- reflect on their own achievements
- respond to other's work

Spelling Development

As with the composing aspects of writing, the secretarial aspects follow a distinct developmental sequence in all children. Nowhere is this clearer than in spelling. Children do not move from initial writing to conventional spelling in one step by dint of rote-learning. A well-established developmental path is trodden with distinct stages as identified by Gentry (1987):

- *A precommunicative stage*: here random letters and numbers, perhaps in strings, are used. There is some knowledge of the alphabet but not of how letters and sounds correspond. Communication requires the presence of the writer to interpret.

- *A semiphonetic stage*: first attempts are now made at letter-sound correspondence. Letter names tend to be used to represent words or parts of words and vowels are usually omitted. Communication is possible with difficulty (e.g. 'camr' for camera, 'lbrte' for liberty).

- *A phonetic stage*: a systematic effort is now made to represent the obvious sound features in words using letter *sounds* rather than names. In addition, visual awareness of spaces and gaps develops. Sounds are represented as pronounced by the writer. (e.g. 'oll' for old, 'weth' for with)

- *A transitional stage*: competence having been developed in representing surface sounds, visual awareness here increases further. The writer begins to recognise and replicate word patterns and some conventional, non-phonetic spellings are produced. Intervention with appropriate teaching strategies which suggest learning procedures will be most effective at this point in the movement from the phonetic to what is sometimes called the morphemic stage. (e.g. 'billdings' for buildings, 'tiyerd' for tired).

- *A correct stage*: now conventional spellings are normally used. A large vocabulary has been memorised and visual memory is well trained to detect any spellings which 'don't look right'. Children have a well-developed awareness of word structures. Misspellings will always be plausible and likely to be ones which literate adults often continue to make.

Spelling in the classroom

It is essential when deciding on classroom strategies to look at children's spelling with this developmental map in mind. In the earliest years when children are operating at the precommunicative and semiphonetic stages the most important consideration will be to receive writing warmly and to respond to the child's content and intentions, so that a positive attitude to writing is fostered and the child wants to keep writing. Correction of secretarial features will be minimal at these early stages.

As children move towards becoming independent writers within a workshop-style organisation, spelling will be attended to along with other transcription features at the editing stage before publication. However all first drafts will have *some* attention given to spelling, just as all final ones are still likely to have a few errors (as all books, including this one, will!). The composing aspect will have priority before the editing stage in a writing workshop and developing writers will be offered procedures for coping with spelling difficulties whilst they compose (such as making informed guesses, using the spelling line for parts of words unsure about, e.g. 'ch ---' for 'child'.) It is important, though, to see these as ways of allowing composition to continue and of avoiding lengthy waits for the teacher to provide correct spellings. They are not intended to be ways of teaching spelling.

Intervention to correct spellings in the editing process will still need to be varied according to the developmental stage of the spellers and their level of confidence. At the phonetic stage, corrections will clearly have to be sensitive and selective otherwise the whole piece of work may end up being rewritten, damaging motivation and self-belief. Commonly used words or words which are close to conventional spellings can profitably be commented on and the correct spelling supplied in the context of written comments, but these need be no more than a few for each piece of writing.

Transitional spellers and children moving out of the phonetic phase will be ready to find and check words for themselves. Working in pairs, they can be encouraged to edit their own and others' work and use appropriate dictionaries and individual and class word collections to correct as much as possible. These self-editing habits will become internalised for the correct stage speller.

Children will also need to be offered methods of learning spellings if they are to develop appropriate habits. Copying spellings from the board or from a teacher's correction, the traditional way, is ineffective. Writing out a word three times is at best handwriting practice. For this reason looking at the appearance of words on the page is important, not having words spelled out letter name by letter name. Correct spellings should always be given by writing out the whole word not by adding or inserting letters into children's writing. Words will need to be spelled from short-term memory, initially.

The 'Look, Cover, Write, Check' technique offers a procedure for just this sort of training. In this method, spellings are always written down and carefully *looked* at first as visual patterns, possibly traced in the air, and then sounded out. Next the spelling is *covered* and the writer tries to reproduce it by remembering and *writing* it. The correct spelling is then revealed again and the word *checked*. If the two do not match the procedure is followed again.

Simple booklets can be produced to encourage the LCWC technique and allow children to use it independently:

The strategy here is to teach children *how* to learn new or difficult spellings rather than emphasising the rote-learning of particular words.

fold		fold	
<u>1st Try</u>	<u>Spellings</u>	<u>2nd Try</u>	
rythm	rhythm	rhythm	
referred	referred		
etc.	etc.	etc.	

As Torbe (1978) has pointed out, the teacher's role is not so much to correct mistakes pupils have already made as to help them not to make that mistake next time.

Alongside this developmental approach to spelling, teachers will also need to foster an interest in and inquisitiveness about words (see also contexts for Language Study in Chapter Four). There are many word games which can support spelling development as well as being enjoyable whole class activities (see Torbe (1978) and Redfern (1993) for examples). Work on dictionary skills, also possibly in the form of games, will be necessary to demonstrate to most children how best to use these, working from initial sounds and letter clusters. Whole class spelling tests can have motivational value but are usually predictable in outcome and fail to provide useful information about individuals. Pair testing can be more effective using lists of words tailored to individual needs and preferably taken from pupils' own writing. These lists can be conveniently compiled on box-file cards as children's writing is being marked. Dictation can also be helpful if used for diagnostic purposes to produce short pieces of writing which can be systematically analysed for patterns of error in a kind of 'miscue analysis'. Short focused sessions drawing attention to spelling patterns, letter strings, prefixes and suffixes, word families and derivations can also be productive, particularly if used alongside a developmental approach to spelling which also values writing as important in the primary classroom.

Punctuation

Like spelling, punctuation is best tackled in the context of children's own writing and their current needs as developing writers. In workshop writing it would again be scrutinised at the editing stage.

Demonstration of the need for punctuation in written communication usually has a motivating effect on young writers. Getting children to read aloud their own writing and compare the pauses, stresses and intonations they insert with the punctuation present on the page is an effective way to achieve this, as the NC suggests (p.9). Matching written punctuation with the prosody of spoken language is a useful starting place, but as with spelling, the writing-speech correspondence is not enough in itself. Speech has pauses and rhythms not marked in written language and punctuation in writing often relates to meaning not speech patterns (Smith, 1982, p.156).

More experienced writers can therefore be challenged to insert punctuation into a suitable passage from a familiar book from which, perhaps, full stops, commas, capital letters and question marks have been deleted. The punctuation marks inserted can then be compared to the original book passage and variation discussed, remembering that sometimes there is room for debate about the need for, say, a comma rather than a full stop and that the punctuation used by authors and publishers can be individual and does change over time (contemporary books tend to include less punctuation than those published 50 years ago and far less than 100 years ago). Looking closely at punctuation in both literary and information texts will give insights into how writers use it to express meaning in ways different from speech.

As with spelling, short structured sessions on aspects of punctuation (e.g. speech marks) for groups or a whole class will be most valuable when related directly to on-going classroom writing (e.g. writing stories with dialogue, writing reports about interviews). Pupil-designed posters or reference sheets which can be attached to writing folders or books are also valuable reinforcements of punctuation points learned. The most valuable motivator of all for consistent punctuation will be course be the presence of real, critical audiences for children's writing.

Handwriting

The links between spelling and handwriting are clearly established. Awareness of letter strings and word patterns develops more quickly once a cursive script ('joined up' writing) has been acquired and kinesthetic memory or 'spelling in the tips of the fingers' is established. For this reason children are now often introduced to cursive writing as soon as possible at KS1 and from the outset are taught to form individual letters with a 'flick' at the end which will be used later for joining them into words. This avoids children having to learn a different way of forming letters when they move from printing to joining up. It is also established practice now to present initial letter sounds in letter formation sequence, that is:

c o a d g q s e (backward formation movement)

r n m p h b u y (forward formation movement)

l t k f i j (vertical formation movement)

v w x z (angular formation movement)

The 1995 NC has this to say about the 'key skill' of handwriting at KS1:

pupils should be taught to hold a pencil comfortably in order to develop a legible style that follows the conventions of written English, including:

- writing from left to right and from top to bottom of the page

- starting and finishing letters correctly

- regularity of size and shape of letters

- regularity of spacing of letters and words

They should be taught the conventional ways of forming letters, both lower case and capitals. They should build on their knowledge of letter formation to join letters in words. They should develop an awareness of the importance of clear and neat presentation, in order to communicate their meaning effectively. (p.10)

At KS2 the programmes of study suggest that pupils should 'be given opportunities to continue to develop legible handwriting in both joined up and printed styles', increasing control and fluency. The idea of appropriateness is emphasised here: 'They should be taught to use different forms of handwriting for different purposes, e.g. *print for labelling maps or diagrams; a clear neat hand for finished, presented work; a faster script for notes'* (p.16).

Rosemary Sassoon (1983) has suggested the following order of priorities for handwriting development:

1. legibility

2. speed

3. a personal hand.

She stresses the highly individual nature of developed handwriting and the variety of factors, physical, psychological and environmental which can affect how we write by hand. Although children will all be taught to follow a model of conventional letter formation at the beginning, individual variations are bound to develop. Whilst allowing for the eventual evolution of the personal hand, checks will need to be made in the classroom not only on letter forms but also on basic techniques such as:

- *pen grip*: ideally this should be a relaxed 'tripod' grip, pen between thumb and index finger and resting against the middle finger (my own idiosyncratic grip, I notice, uses the middle finger also to hold the pen!). The pen or pencil should be a comfortable thickness for the child's fingers

- *seating posture*: this needs to be reasonably straight, with the writing surface at a comfortable height and in sufficient light, and with the writing arm properly supported

- *paper positioning*: this will be different for left and right handers. Paper should be to the left or right of the body-line as appropriate, usually angled at about 45 degrees. For this reason left handers and right handers should not be seated side by side in such a way that their writing arms will clash

Debate about the type of paper children should write on has apparently been going on for about 400 years! (Jarman, 1979 p.19). In practice unlined paper is generally used for children in the initial stages of concentrating on letter formation and hand movements. Once these are established and children are beginning to join letters, lined paper with a sufficiently wide gap between baselines is introduced. Unlined paper with ruled guidelines placed underneath so as to show through is often used in primary schools, particularly where handwritten work is produced for visual display or made into books and where handwriting is valued as a craft activity.

Legible, fast and personal handwriting, like the other secretarial skills, will develop most effectively within purposeful writing contexts where pride in the writer's own work links with a respect for the needs of the reader.

The Assessment of Writing

It might be best to begin by defining terms in an area where terminology can often be confusing:

- *Responding*: this relatively recent term tends to refer to the more continuous written and oral comments a teacher makes on or about a particular piece of writing. The response would be addressed to the child, possibly inviting a dialogue, would be positive in tenor and reacting firstly to the content of the work. The one-word evaluation comments and grading systems of traditional 'marking' would be avoided. Correction of transcription errors would be selective and constructive rather than a mechanical proof-reading.

- *Assessing*: this refers to the measuring of children's achievements in writing either against a checklist of agreed qualities ('criterion-referenced') or against other children's work and what is considered normal for the child's age ('norm-referenced'). The purpose of assessing can be either 'formative', *to inform* the teacher's future planning by providing diagnostic information, or 'summative', *to sum up* a child's attainment at a given point in order to report to the parents, other teachers or schools, local or national authorities.

- *Profiling*: this consists of the recording of formative comments on a child's achievements which seeks to give a more rounded picture of development over time than the traditional end of term school report. Profiles might include comments from children themselves and possibly from their parents (as in the *Primary Language Record*). A 'portfolio' of children's written work might also be included.

(i) **Responding**

How children's work is received both in spoken and written feedback is crucial in forming their perceptions of writing. However much the processes of writing are apparently valued in the classroom, if the reception of the product concentrates on secretarial correctness primarily, then this is the aspect which children will perceive as the most important.

Feedback which regularly consists of 'a tick and a *good*', or even weaker praise than that, can have a subtle demoralising effect. A considered teacher response needs to keep in mind the nature of the writing task and its objectives. What particular skills, understanding and knowledge was it intended to develop? Response should consider how far these objectives were achieved and how the writer might develop them further. As has already been said, purposeful writing for specific readerships must also receive response which reflects its fitness for the purpose, audience and form chosen, and include feedback, critical or congratulatory, from its intended readers.

As well as appropriate responses from others, children need to evaluate periodically their own writing and their progress. If entirely dependent on teacher response, young writers are less likely to develop a critical stance towards their own and others' writing; an important form of awareness in writing development.

(ii) Assessing

Writing is always bound by the context of the particular task (paragraphing cannot be assessed in poems, for example). For this reason, assessment always needs to be based on a cumulative appreciation of children's achievements in a variety of different kinds of writing over time. Development in writing, just as in oracy and in reading, is not linear but recursive, with writers repeatedly returning to the task of orchestrating a complex of skills all at different stages of development, rather than moving on step by step from one discrete skill to the next.

The 1995 NC offer descriptions of writing attainment in the primary years at five levels, inviting teachers to match pupils up to the general picture which 'best fits', even if not all parts of the description are equally appropriate. To some extent this procedure recognises the difficult of fitting writing attainment into a linear model of assessment. The descriptions given at each level cover the following main aspects of writing:

- communication of meaning
- awareness of audience and purpose
- appropriate use of form and style
- vocabulary choice
- grammatical structures
- spelling
- punctuation
- handwriting

If the first four aspects are taken together as composing features of writing, the Level Descriptions can be analysed into five main strands for the purposes of looking at suggested progression (level 6 is added for reference):

AT3 WRITING: LEVEL DESCRIPTIONS

Composing Features

level 1: Pupils' writing communicates meaning through simple words and phrases.

level 2: Pupils' writing communicates meaning in both narrative and non-narrative forms, using appropriate and interesting vocabulary, and showing some awareness of the reader.

level 3: Pupils' writing is often organised, imaginative and clear. The main features of different forms of writing are used appropriately, beginning to be adapted to different readers. Sequences of sentences extend ideas logically and words are chosen for variety and interest.

level 4: Pupils' writing in a range of forms is lively and thoughtful. Ideas are often sustained and developed in interesting ways and organised appropriately for the purpose and the reader. Vocabulary choices are often adventurous and words are used for effect.

level 5: Pupils' writing is varied and interesting, conveying meaning clearly in a range of forms for different readers, using a more formal style where appropriate. Vocabulary choices are imaginative and words are used precisely.

level 6: Pupils' writing often engages and sustains the reader's interest, showing some adaptation of style and register to different forms, including using an impersonal style where appropriate.

Grammatical Features

level 3: The basic grammatical structure of sentences is usually correct.

level 4: Pupils are beginning to use grammatically complex sentences, extending meaning.

level 5: Simple and complex sentences are organised into paragraphs.

level 6: Pupils use a range of sentence structures and varied vocabulary to create effects.

Spelling

level 2: Simple monosyllabic words are usually spelt correctly, and where there are inaccuracies the alternative is phonetically plausible.

level 3: Spelling is usually accurate, including that of common, polysyllabic words.

level 4: Spelling, including that of polysyllabic words that conform to regular patterns, is generally accurate.

level 5: Words with complex regular patterns are usually spelt correctly.

level 6: Spelling is generally accurate, including that of irregular words.

Punctuation

level 1: In their reading or their writing, pupils begin to show awareness of how full stops are used.

level 2: Ideas are developed in a sequence of sentences, sometimes demarcated by capital letters and full stops.

level 3: Punctuation to mark sentences -- full stops, capital letters and question marks -- is used accurately.

level 4: Full stops, capital letters and question marks are used correctly, and pupils are beginning to use puntuation within the sentence.

level 5: A range of punctuation, including commas, apostrophes and inverted commas, is usually used accurately.

level 6: A range of punctuation is usually used correctly to clarify meaning, and ideas are organised into paragraphs.

Handwriting

level 1: Letters are usually clearly shaped and correctly orientated.

level 2: In handwriting, letters are accurately formed and consistent in size.

level 3: Handwriting is joined and legible.

level 4: Handwriting style is fluent, joined and legible.

level 5: Handwriting is joined, clear and fluent and, where appropriate, is adapted to a range of tasks.

level 6: Handwriting is neat and legible.

(iii) **Profiling**

The profile sheet overleaf can be used in conjunction with the level description strands to build up a record of a child's writing over time. It is suggested that it should be used periodically but regularly (once or twice each half-term?) to record observations on a varied sample of children's written work. Ideally the profile would be filed alongside a portfolio of the child's writing compiled over the school year, with some written reflections by the child included too (see page 98).

Further Reading

Beard, R. (1984) *Children's Writing in the Primary School.* London: Edward Arnold.

Czerniewska, P. (1992) *Learning About Writing.* Oxford: Blackwell.

National Writing Project (1989) *Becoming A Writer.* Walton-on-Thames: Nelson.

National Writing Project (1989) *Audiences For Writing.* Walton-on-Thames: Nelson.

National Writing Project (1989) *Writing and Learning.* Walton-on-Thames: Nelson.

Gregory, A., Keiner, J., Lyons, H., and Redfern, A. (1990) *Writers' Workshop.* Stoke-on-Trent: Trentham Books.

Redfern A. and Edwards V. (1990)*Young Authors At Work: Writing 3-13.* University of Reading: Reading and Language Information Centre.

Profile of Writing Achievement

CHILD'S NAME: CLASS: AGE:

DATES

WRITING
ACTIVITY
(inc. Audience,
Purpose, Form)

COMPOSING
FEATURES
(inc. Meaning,
Awareness of
Audience,
Use of form,
style and
vocabulary)

GRAMMATICAL
FEATURES
(inc. Sentence
structure)

SECRETARIAL
FEATURES
(inc. Spelling,
Punctuation,
Handwriting)

OTHER
COMMENTS
(inc. Attitude,
Confidence,
Special Needs)
+ POINTS TO DEVELOP

Chapter Four

STANDARD ENGLISH AND LANGUAGE STUDY

The Background

Before the 1960s Language Study in schools was synonymous with the study of sentence grammar, and associated with activities such as naming the parts of speech (nouns, adjectives, etc.) and analysing artificially-constructed clauses and sentences. My own grammar school exercise book yields the following examples, all marked correct:

Subject	Verb	Object
1. A butcher	sells	meat
2. This box	contains	a large sum of money
3. you	do want	how many pen nibs

When the validity of this mechanistic approach and its effectiveness in transferring skills to children's own writing was challenged in the early 1960s, it was discontinued in many schools. Where this happened, a gap was created in the English curriculum which was often not satisfactorily filled, particularly in the primary school where alternative initiatives such as *Language in Use* (Doughty et al, 1971) and *Language Awareness* (Hawkins, 1987) had less impact.

The *Bullock Report* of 1975 briefly discussed what it called 'Language Study' (11.15-11.40), concluding that 'children should learn about language by experiencing it and experimenting with its use' and reaffirming that the traditional prescriptive study of grammar was ineffective. But it was the HMI discussion paper *Curriculum Matters I* (1984) which reopened the debate and reacted to concern that many children were encountering *no* form of language study by introducing as an explicit aim of English that all pupils should be taught *'about language'*. In a clear anticipation of the National Curriculum the document proposed age-related objectives for 'learning about language' at 11 and 16. The result of many teachers' dissatisfaction with these objectives, expressed in *Responses to Curriculum Matters* (1986), led to the enquiry into English Language teaching which produced the *Kingman Report* (1988). Here the term 'knowledge about language' (KAL) was first used and a model of language constructed to 'inform professional discussion' of it. The model had four equal parts:

Part 1: The forms of the English language

Part 2: Communication and comprehension

Part 3: Acquisition and development

Part 4: Historical and geographical variation

KAL was to cover experience and understanding of *any* of these aspects of English — not simply grammatical forms — though the model was never intended for classroom use. The *Kingman Report* gave examples of practice in primary schools and commented:

> 'Knowledge about language' is not a separate component of the primary or secondary curriculum. It should not be 'bolted on', but should inform children's talking, writing, reading and listening in the classroom. (p48)

Kingman recommended levels of attainment for KAL at 7, 11 and 16, setting these out in two parallel columns, one set referring to pupil performance (implicit KAL), the other to understanding or reflection (explicit KAL).

The Cox Report in 1989 incorporated these recommendations into the design of NC English and defined KAL as covering:

- language variation according to situation, purpose, language mode, regional or social group, etc.

- language in literature

- language variation across time (6.16-6.21)

Following Kingman's advice, KAL was not 'bolted on' as a separate Attainment Target for English (as it was in *Curriculum Matters)* but integrated throughout the ATs for Speaking and Listening, Reading and Writing. It was recognised also that: 'The form in which knowledge about language is communicated will vary with the age and ability of the pupil, from play activities in the pre-school to explicit systematic knowledge in upper secondary education.' Assessment began only at level 5, the upper end of the KS2 attainment range.

The Language in the National Curriculum (LINC) Project (1989-92) was set up to support the implementation of English in the NC in the light of the views of language outlined in the Kingman and Cox Reports. The LINC project deliberately emphasised the third and fourth parts of the Kingman model over the first and second in its attempts to meet the classroom needs of teachers and pupils. So 'language variation' was the main concern, with the 'forms of language' including grammar addressed within that context only. The LINC 'Materials for Professional Development' were never made available directly to schools because of the Government's disagreement with the outcomes of LINC's approach. A lot of valuable development work by LINC was, however, done at local level by various consortia and materials generated from classroom work in these regions have now been made available nationally through commercial publication (Bain et al., 1992, Carter, 1990, Harris and Wilkinson, 1990, Haynes, 1992).

Possibly because of the suppression of the LINC materials, primary teachers were often unclear about precisely what constituted KAL. However the evidence is that the incorporation of this area into the 1989 English NC *did* significantly raise the profile of the study of language in primary classrooms, rescuing it from that period of neglect since the decline of traditional grammar teaching. *NC English: The Case for Revising the Order* (NCC, 1992) commented:

The inclusion of this [KAL] strand has resulted in more attention being paid to Knowledge about Language... Nevertheless... KS1 teachers believe 'that the KAL thread in the English Order needs to be signalled much more clearly than it is at present.' (p.7)

The initial proposals for revising NC English which came out in 1993 dismayed many teachers by omitting KAL almost entirely, with the exception of statements about grammar at KS1 and 2. The *use* of Standard English, there defined as 'the correct use of vocabulary and grammar', was made a much more important feature of the curriculum as the broader KAL was correspondingly reduced.

Encouragingly the 1995 NC for English, produced after further consultation, partially reinstates KAL as 'Language Study' (harking back to Bullock?). This strand is certainly now more clearly signposted, being a named section of the Programmes of Study for all three Attainment Targets at each Key Stage. Originally the English advisory group had proposed 'Language Study and Standard English' as the title of this section, but this was altered before publication to 'Standard English and Language Study' (*TES* 13 May, 1994), suggesting the greater prominence still given to the former than in the 1989 NC.

It is still stressed, however, that activities within this area, as with all other areas of English, should take place 'within integrated programmes of speaking and listening, reading and writing', as Kingman and Cox recommended. The design of the English curriculum discourages approaching Standard English and Language Study separately as a 'bolt-on' component. A separate section has been devoted to this area here because it is still an underdeveloped aspect of primary English teaching and a cause of some confusion and anxiety. However, the approach suggested and the activities mentioned will be seen to fit in naturally with those put forward in earlier chapters.

The dispute over the title of this section in the NC may be seen as part of a wider debate between a cultural heritage view of English and language, which seeks to transmit values unchanged, and a cultural analysis view, which seeks to equip children to examine them critically, to use terms referred to in the Introduction. Should the use and appreciation of Standard English be set within the wider critical and reflective context of

Language Study, or should the purpose of Language Study be mainly to increase and improve children's use of Standard English? The opportunities suggested below for developing Standard English and Language Study will offer a broad and descriptive approach which seeks to interrelate the requirements of this section with those of the 'Range' and 'Key Skills' section of the NC for English.

Contexts for Standard English and Language Study

Richard Bain (1991) has suggested a model for learning about language in the classroom which might be set out diagrammatically as follows:

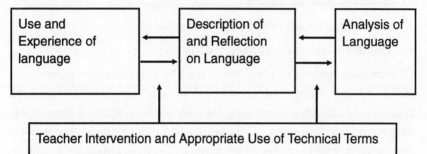

As this model suggests, enabling children to describe and reflect on their experience of language, the middle stage of this process, is the crucial feature of Language Study in the primary years. Formal analysis with appropriate metalanguage may or may not follow reflection at this stage: it certainly need not follow automatically. What is important is the raising of awareness of language and the anchoring of both reflection and any analysis in the ground of real experience. This can only happen effectively through appropriate teacher intervention, as indicated in the learning process.

Bain (1991) also suggests three levels at which teachers can intervene in the classroom to promote Language Study:

- by reflection on language in use in the classroom

- through planned contexts for more sharply focused reflection

- through explicit language investigations

Reflection on Language in Use

Here the 'opportunities to reflect on their use of language' (p16) which the NC requires for primary pupils occur incidentally not systematically or comprehensively. They can arise out of any aspect of the school day. It requires teachers to be aware of language in use and alert to possible learning points. Opportunities for arousing curiosity about language use might arise, for example, from:

- topical news items involving language
- pupils' own news items
- assembly talks by visitors
- new words, names or phrases encountered
- children's television, comics or magazines

Often stories, poems or plays being read by individuals or groups will throw up interesting and unexpected uses of language: a character speaking in dialect, a poem with onomatopoeic words or a play which uses American expressions. Topic work will present many likely contexts: children constructing an interview sheet will have an opportunity to think about how best to frame questions to elicit a useful response.

However the most common incidental context for reflection on language in the classroom will be during the discussion of children's own reading and writing, and occasionally their speaking and listening. Talking about a piece of writing in draft with individuals, pairs or groups provides an ideal occasion to develop children's understanding of how language works and to equip them with the appropriate terms to describe it. What better time to raise awareness of joining words than during a writing conference about a story which uses only 'and' or 'then' to connect phrases and sentences ? Or to reflect on the power of adjectives than during the reading of a poem which uses them sparingly? Insights are also available during these discussions into the nature of written language as compared to spoken and how the two complementary modes vary in form and function. Any technical terms used should be an immediately useful device for children to gain a perspective on their own and others' usage, encouraging them to see language as a system which can be manipulated and which empowers the reflective user.

Planned Contexts for Standard English

Reliance on incidental learning only will clearly not meet pupil needs or NC requirements in terms of Standard English and Language Study. Contexts will also need to be planned and organised, but these can still arise out of the integrated English programme the NC refers to and need not be decontextualised skills exercises only.

The NC requires that: 'Pupils should be given opportunities to develop' both their 'understanding' and 'use' of standard English (p3) and 'should be introduced with appropriate sensitivity to the importance of standard English' (p5). Standard English is here defined not as 'correct English' but as 'distinguished from other forms of English by its vocabulary and by rules and conventions of grammar, spelling and punctuation'. It is recognised that there are differences between the written and spoken forms. It is also made clear that 'spoken standard English is not the same as Received Pronunciation and can be expressed in a variety of accents'. The programmes of study go further and point out that: 'The richness of dialects and other languages can make an important contribution to pupils' knowledge and understanding of standard English' (p2).

Pupils' reading can again provide an effective way into this area. Class novels or stories can be specifically chosen for their language interest and for the language activities they might give rise to (as well as for their qualities as narratives!). Let's look at one classroom where such a planned context is being used:

A Y5 class are reading *A Tea-Leaf on the Roof* by Jean Ure (1987). The book was selected partly because of the way it plays on children's awareness of different varieties of language and their knowledge of literary conventions to give a new twist to the stock adventure story of children's literature. William's father is a professional writer of children's fiction, writing under the pen name 'Justin Case' about an Enid Blyton-like gang led by 'Alistair'. William and his own rather different gang get involved in the hunt for a Cockney-speaking thief (the 'tea-leaf' of the title) who is stealing lead from the roofs of their run-down terrace.

As part of their response to reading the novel, the class are involved in role-playing characters from the book:

- William's gang: Mash Khan, the 'butch' Charlotte and her younger sister Geraldine

- Alistair's gang: 'plump' Porky, 'tiny' Spickanspan, Eliza and Dorothy who 'behaved properly, as girls should'

- Chalky, the thief, who speaks in rhyming slang

- the 'Jogger', the children's chief suspect, who tries to 'talk posh'

- the children's parents

These characters take part in improvised conversations with each other in situations arising from the story. They also take part in more formal interviews with other children playing the parts of:

- police officers

- various journalists

- various television or radio reporters

At the end of the role-playing the children will be asked to reflect on how they spoke in character. They will describe this in pairs at first following a number of prompts such as:

- How did you speak?

- Why did you speak like that?

- Did you use any special words?

- Did you say any words in a special way?

When the discussion moves to a whole class one the teacher will prompt comparisons such as:

- What differences were there between William's way of speaking and Alistair's?

- Between Charlotte's and Dorothy's?

- How did Chalky speak differently from the Jogger?

- How did the BBC interviewer speak?

To facilitate these comparisons the teacher will go on to introduce the terms 'accent', 'dialect' and 'standard English', relating them to terms used in previous sessions such as 'register' (that is, how language varies according to context, audience and purpose), 'diction' and 'intonation'.

Definitions will not be offered at this stage, only examples. The children will be invited to mention other situations in their experience where an accent, dialect or standard English might have been used, such as on television.

As the reading of the novel continues this area of language diversity will be explored further and extended by considering speakers whose repertoire might include two or more languages, such as Mash Khan. Written language will also be investigated by comparing the stylistic features of different types of text: an Enid Blyton 'Secret Seven' or 'Famous Five' novel compared to Jean Ure's, for instance.

If children are to 'appreciate' as well as use standard English, they will need to encounter situations such as these where they can 'consider their own speech and how they communicate with others' (NC p5) through a distancing device such as role-play. If the understanding of standard English is to be developed within the broader frame of Language Study, standard English will need to be experienced alongside other varieties, so that children can 'investigate how language varies according to context and purpose and between standard and dialect forms' (p12).

Other novels which could be used in this way include:

- *Thunder and Lightnings,* Jan Mark (1976)
- *The Secret Garden,* Frances Hodgson Burnett (1911)
- *George Speaks,* Dick King-Smith (1988)

Other planned opportunities for developing awareness of spoken and standard English in the context of language diversity might be:

- imaginary telephone conversations with a variety of speakers
- sales assistant-customer conversations in the classroom shop (or estate agency, travel agents, newsagents, etc.)
- simulations of television and radio programmes such as national and local news, weather forecasts, chat shows, etc
- exercises in mixing up language varieties (East Enders performed in RP; the news read in RAP; a teacher speaking teenage slang, etc.)
- comparing children's television programmes of the 1950s and 60s with equivalent ones today

- preparing a debate on a World Standard Language for the 21st century

The features and functions of *written* standard English could be approached by related activities such as:

- compiling dialect dictionaries

- groups tape-recording conversations and attempting to transcribe those of other groups

- 'translating' a piece of dialect writing into standard English

- 'translating' a well-known piece of literature into dialect or slang

- writing a report based on a taped interview

- writing a television or radio news script

- looking at different varieties of written language in the letters of *The Jolly Postman.*

Planned Contexts for Language Study

Storytelling and reading will also provide opportunities for sharply focused reflection on other areas of language. Myths, legends, folk tales and fables concerned with different aspects of language occur in all cultures and provide a fascinating introduction to language study for a wide age-range. Stories from the Bible such as the Creation and Adam's naming of every living creature (Genesis chs 1 and 2), the Tower of Babel (ch 11) and the 'Shibboleth' test (Judges ch 12) encourage reflection on the mysterious origins of language. Stories from other traditions can readily be found too, for instance:

- 'The Word the Devil Made Up', in *Afro-American Folktales*, ed R.D. Abrahams (1985)

- 'The Man Who Learned the Language of Animals', in *African Myths and Legends*, retold by K. Arnott (1962)

Aesop's fables provide the origin for many popular phrases and sayings, such as 'sour grapes' ('The Fox and the Grapes'), 'crying wolf' ('The Shepherd Boy and the Wolf') or 'wolf in sheep's clothing'. Folk and fairy tales like 'Rumpelstiltskin' also have many examples of the power of words, names and repetitive patterns of language.

Words and Meanings

Many of these stories provide a ready way into the topic of words and meanings which is a prominent part of Language Study in the NC. Novels, picture books and poems are again a valuable resource, for example:

- 'Jabberwocky', Lewis Carroll (invented words and names)
- *The BFG* (1982), Roald Dahl (invented words and names)
- *The TV Kid* (1976), Betsy Byars (American English)
- *Dr Xargle's Book of Earth Tiggers* (1990), Jeanne Willis and Tony Ross (alien definitions of familiar words and things)

The approach should be one which encourages curiosity, enthusiasm *and* a critical stance towards language. This should be the case even with activities which are deliberately designed to extend vocabulary by investigating particular types of words:

- synonyms (words which are similar in meaning)
- antonyms (words which are opposite in meaning)
- homophones (words which sound the same but have different meanings and spellings, eg *ceiling/sealing*)
- homonyms (words which sound and look the same but have different meanings, eg *cricket*, meaning both an insect and a ball game).

Critical scrutiny would ask: *is* there such a thing as a true synonym or antonym? If part of the meaning of all words are the associations and connotations that surround them (word association games can easily reveal these) can any two words really be the same or opposite? And what is the use of a thesaurus in that case?

The same is true of activities designed to support spelling by investigating word families and letter strings. An investigative approach which equips children to describe and reflect will foster Language Study, rather than a prescriptive approach which simply presents children with the results of analysis.

Investigations into words and meanings can also involve:

- words used by particular groups of people (children, teachers, sports personalities, politicians, etc.)

- words used in particular jobs or professions (estate agents, travel agents, lawyers, advertising)
- words used in particular subjects (Maths, Science, Music, Art, Geography, History)
- words use in stories and in poetry
- words used in jokes and puns
- words seen in the local environment
- word origins
- changes in words and meanings over time
- differences in words and meanings between places
- new words and meanings
- slang words
- code words

Word games are another effective strategy. These can focus on the internal structure of words — as with Word Ladders (making one word into another by changing a letter at a time, e.g. *CAT,* COT, DOT, *DOG*) or Shannon's Game (a hangman-type game which involves guessing letters in words). Alternatively they can focus on meaning — as with Elephant and Elbow, where the challenge is to provide a word which has no connection in meaning with the one previously given, or the opposite, to provide a word connected in meaning in some way (e.g. Elephant, Castle, Rook, Pigeon, etc.). Players have to be able to justify their choices or objections in the event of being challenged! Many other examples of similar activities can be found in *Word Games* by Sandy Brownjohn and Janet Whitaker (1995).

Commercially available card or board games involving word-play can also be valuable, such as:

- Junior Scrabble
- Junior Dingbats
- Countdown (from the television series)
- Dictionary Dice

Computer programs also provide language games which can help to stimulate awareness of words and meanings, for instance:

- WORDPLAY
- TRAY.

IT's English (NATE, 1990) discusses the use of these and other IT resources for language awareness (see Chapter 5).

Finally, encouraging children to invent their own games based on words and meanings, and to play them, will be a natural extension of using the ones mentioned above.

Grammar

Word games can also be a successful strategy for approaching the other area of Language Study referred to specifically in the NC, grammar. Here the term is being used to refer to syntax and discourse structure, the system of forming phrases, clauses, sentences and paragraphs, rather than in the larger sense of 'all we know about a language'. (An investigation into what different people think the word 'grammar' itself means is a fruitful topic for older children, and for teachers!).

Games allow children to build on their use and experience of grammar, their implicit knowledge about language, and allow teachers to introduce terms and concepts, as appropriate, which enable children to describe and reflect on that usage. These games can develop from ones popular with younger children such as 'I Spy' (where the answer will usually be a noun), 'The Minister's Cat' (adjectives) or 'When Jenny/Billy was in the nursery/infants, she/he...' (verbs).

The following guessing game usually proves addictive with 9-11 year olds and can be adapted for younger juniors:

1. Teacher or child thinks of a sentence with 10 words (children's sentences may need to be vetted beforehand!)

2. Each word is indicated by a line on the board or large sheet of paper (_____ _____ _____ etc.)

3. The other children have 5 guesses at each word.

4. They may 'hold' after 4 guesses on one word *only* at a time and then go on to the next word, returning to the word on 'hold' when they have built up a context for a final guess.

5. If the word is correctly guessed within 5 turns, the guessing team gain a point. If the word is not guessed, the sentence- maker gains the point. The winner is the one with most points out of 10.

6. Clues are given about the words to be guessed which point the guessers towards the grammatical patterns of sentences rather than the meanings of the words (e.g. joining word; 'says where/when/how' etc.; article; preposition; etc.)

Grammar games which exploit the patterning, word-play and linguistic inventiveness of poetry can be used to focus attention, within the context of children's own writing, on particular classes of words which the NC suggests children should be 'taught to use' , and presumably to understand, at KS2: nouns, pronouns, adjectives, prepositions, conjunctions and verb tenses (p.16). So, for example, Sandy Brownjohn suggests how poems can be constructed around the use of adverbs, prepositions, collective nouns or verbs. In *To Rhyme or Not to Rhyme?* (1994) she includes these and many other activities which support both language study and poetry writing and suggests other poetry games teachers could devise themselves (can you write a conjunctions poem?).

Using the same strategy of combining a game element with poetry activities it's possible to move on to a more analytical approach to word classes and sentence structure. Brownjohn recommends the word game played by the Surrealist poets called 'The Exquisite Corpse'. Here each player has a sheet of paper divided into vertical columns headed:

Adjective/Adjective/Noun/Verb/Adverb/Adjective/Adjective/Noun

These can of course be varied as appropriate. Players write down 4-5 entries in the first column, fold back the paper to conceal these and pass on the sheet for the next player to complete the next column. This continues until all the columns are completed and the papers can be unfolded. The resulting bizarre (but grammatical) sentences can be read out and discussed, with articles, prepositions, verb tenses added or altered as necessary. They can then be used for nonsense poems. The computer program WORDPLAY will generate structurally identical sentences in a similar way, but without the hilarious incongruities.

A simplified version of this grammar poetry can be played orally with children by getting them to think of an adjective and a noun beginning with the same letter ('angry alligators'), or an adjective, noun and verb ('angry alligators amble'), or an adjective, noun, verb and adverb ('angry alligators amble agitatedly'), and so on. The speed and complexity (e.g. using alphabetical order) can again be varied as desired. Grammatical terms can be discussed beforehand, learnt through the game or not used if inappropriate.

More complex sentence structures can be explored with older children through other practical activities. For example, children can be challenged to expand simple sentences ('Old Macdonald had a farm') into complex ones by adding on phrases and clauses ('Despite his age', 'so his friends say', 'although he was a vegetarian', 'and hated noise', etc.). This will work best if the basic elements of the initial sentence (*subject*: 'Old Macdonald'; *verb*: 'had'; *complement or object*: 'a farm') as well as the add-on phrases and clauses are cut up and mounted on card. Conjunctions can be mounted separately, and divided into co-ordinating (and, or, but, etc.) and subordinating ones (although, so, etc.). In this way the sentence structure can easily be manipulated and interchangeable resources built up. As usual, technical terms need only be used if appropriate. Discussion of sentences produced, grammatical and ungrammatical, is vital, including consideration of when simple sentences are more effective stylistically. Phrases, clauses and sentences related to pupils' own writing could also be used for this activity (see Hunt, 1994 for further ideas).

Structure beyond the sentence level can be investigated in active ways too. Using highlighter pens of different colours, children can identify the *cohesive ties* which bind sentences together into coherent longer passages of writing. This could involve looking at conjunctions used to link sentences in ways which indicate a relationship to what has gone before. There are four main sorts:
- Temporal (after, then, earlier, etc.)
- Causal (thus, therefore, so, etc.)
- Additive (moreover, furthermore etc.)
- Adversative (however, but, nevertheless, etc.)

Other cohesive ties could also be highlighted: words such as pronouns (he, she, etc) and articles (the, an, a) used to refer back to previous words; or similar words used to substitute for ones already used. For example:

Once upon a time there lived *an ugly prince*. *He* wished to be turned into **a beautiful frog**. One day a princess kissed *him* and changed *the young man* into **just such a creature**. **It** hopped into a pond and lived happily ever after.

The most manageable way to approach this activity is for children to choose one element in the passage ('prince' or 'frog' as marked here, but also 'time' or 'change') and to follow the chain of references and substitutions which run through the text. The *lexical chains* might also be picked out in this way: these are words related by meaning and usage which combine together to give the writing further cohesion. Here, for example, there is a lexical chain of words related to the genre of fairy tales ('Once upon a time', 'prince', 'princess', 'frog', 'lived happily ever after'). Discussion of cohesion can also consider texts which are difficult to read because they lack appropriate ties or which set up expectations (like the above) which they then subvert. Enjoyable writing activities can be devised to produce texts of these kinds.

Language Investigations

Aspects of Standard English and Language Study lend themselves well to being the organising focus for large-scale cross- curricular topics in the primary school.

Let's look at a class involved in one such investigation.

A Y2 class are following a half-term's topic on 'Names and Naming'. Beginning with the children's own names and those of family and friends the class have investigated the origin and meaning of first names and surnames, compiling their own computer data-base from the findings. They have discussed how spellings of names vary, how names can be shortened, how nicknames evolve and why people change their names. Using information books, they have looked at the popularity of first names at different times and conducted a survey of parents' and grandparents' names, presenting their results in tables and charts. At the moment they are involved in making a class book of stories containing invented names for characters, animals and places, using their knowledge of naming gained so far.

They will go on to consider names and naming practices in different cultures, acting out some of these and bringing to the classroom mementoes from their own name-giving ceremonies. Finally the topic will focus on names in the local environment: common local surnames from churchyards, the names of local schools, streets, shops, businesses and houses, and how these came about. Maps, drawings and letter-writing will result from this particular facet of the topic.

The links with other KS1 programmes of study for NC subjects are clear here. For example:

- Geography: fieldwork in the locality of the school
- History: change in children's own lives and that of their family
- IT: communicating and handling information
- Maths: collecting, recording and interpreting data
- RE: ceremonies in different religions

The following language-based topics also have potential for cross-curricular work:

- Communication (Design and Technology, IT, Geography, History, Science)
- Writing (Art, Design and Technology, History, IT)
- Books (Art, Design and Technology, History, IT)
- Languages (History, Geography, IT)

Topic work in other curriculum subjects will also yield plenty of opportunities for language investigations. History-based topics are a particularly fruitful area. All the NC Study Units at KS2 have elements of language study within them:

- Ancient Egypt (hieroglyphs)
- Ancient Greece (influence of language on modern world)
- Romans, Anglo-Saxons and Vikings in Britain (influences on the English language and on personal and place names)

- Life in Tudor times (Shakespeare's language)
- Victorian Britain (Dickens' language)
- Britain since 1930 (language change over time)
- Local History (dialect, accent, names)

Geography-based topics which concentrate on two contrasting localities also have plenty of potential for language investigations -- looking at different languages or scripts by comparing the UK with an African or Asian country (e.g. Ghana or China) or with a South American or Central American/Caribbean one (e.g. Peru or Jamaica).

The vocabularies of *all* the different curriculum subjects, in particular the language of Art, Music, Maths and Science, are also areas where Language Study can be pursued across the curriculum, and the NC programmes of study emphasise the importance of appropriate subject vocabulary to children's learning in these areas.

Finally within the English curriculum itself, of course, there is plentiful scope for longer language investigations into areas already mentioned, such as:

- differences between speech and writing
- accents, dialects and standard English
- the language of literature
- language change

As in all primary topic work the aim in these language investigations would be to discover the extent of children's existing awareness, to utilise that and to enable them to explore further, using appropriate resources and fieldwork, collecting and collating data and selecting effective means of presenting what is found out. Within this the NC programmes of study will be a framework to help planning and assessment but not a strait-jacket to limit inquiry.

Monitoring And Assessment

The inclusion of Standard English and Language Study as an explicit strand in English in the 1995 NC will make it necessary for primary teachers to ensure coverage and progression in this area in a more deliberate way even than under the 1989 curriculum. Varied contexts will need to be devised and organised to maintain broad, integrated experiences of language work throughout the primary years.

In the earlier NC, knowledge about language did not appear in the assessment schedule until level 5, the upper limit of the primary range, which many teachers felt to be too late. It was never assessed by way of separate SATs but always as part of teacher assessment of ongoing English work in the classroom.

Language Study does not appear at all in the 1995 Level Descriptions. However, children's awareness and use of standard English does appear as a strand in AT1, Speaking and Listening, where attainment is plotted along the following scale:

Level 1:   (no reference)

Level 2:   Pupils are beginning to be aware that in some situations a more formal vocabulary and tone of voice are used.

Level 3:   They are beginning to be aware of standard English and when it is used.

Level 4:   They use appropriately some of the features of standard English vocabulary and grammar.

Level 5:   They begin to use standard English in formal situations.

Level 6:   They are usually fluent in their use of standard English in formal situations.

Again it needs to be remembered that the level descriptions are holistic statements rather than accumulations of discrete strands. However, this still means that teachers will need to flesh out the full picture of their children's knowledge about language by placing this awareness and use of standard English within the larger context of overall achievement in Language Study resulting from the kinds of activities and opportunities suggested in this chapter.

Further Reading

Bain, R. (1991) *Reflections: Talking About Language.* London: Hodder and Stoughton.

Bain, R. Fitzgerald, B. and Taylor, M. (1992) [eds] *Looking into Language.* London: Hodder and Stoughton.

Brownjohn, S. and Gwyn-Jones, G. (1995) *Spotlight on the English Language.* London: Hodder and Stoughton.

Carter, R. (1990) [ed] *Knowledge about Language and the Curriculum.* London: Hodder and Stoughton.

Haynes, J. (1991) *A Sense of Words.* London: Hodder and Stoughton.

Houlton, D. (1985) *All Our Languages.* London: Edward Arnold.

Hunt, G. (1994) *Inspirations for Grammar.* Leamington Spa: Scholastic.

Lutrario, C. (1994) *Exploring Language.* Aylesbury: Ginn 1994.

Raleigh, M. (1981) *The Languages Book.* London: The English and Media Centre.

Chapter Five

INFORMATION TECHNOLOGY AND MEDIA EDUCATION

The Background

> Round the city of Caxton, the electronic suburbs are rising. To the language of books is added the language of television and radio, the elliptical demotic of the telephone, the processed codes of the computer. As the shapes of literacy multiply, so our dependence on language *increases* (para. 2.7, my emphasis).

This quotation from the *Kingman Report* (1988) vividly describes the new literacies which confront children and teachers at the end of the 20th century, presenting challenges as well as opportunities. It neatly links the two areas which form the subject of this chapter, suggesting the close interrelatedness of the computer and the other electronic media such as television, radio, the telephone and fax machine, all of which properly come under the heading of 'Information Technology'. It has become more common however, to refer to teaching and learning about television and radio in particular as 'Media Education'. The paragraph from *Kingman*, an enquiry into the teaching of English Language, also stresses how, contrary to popular belief, the rise of new communication technologies actually *increases* our dependence on language in spoken and written form. They make it more necessary that children should be confident, reflective and critical users of language if they are to be inhabitants of the suburbs which are rising *now* around the city of print: not new cities, but extensions of the existing literacy domains.

Kingman points out how literacy in the fullest sense is and will remain central to our whole social and political order:

> People need expertise in language to be able to participate effectively in a democracy. There is no point in having access to information that you cannot understand, or having the opportunity to propose policies that you cannot formulate.... A democratic society needs people who have the linguistic abilities which will enable them to discuss, evaluate and make sense of what they are told, as well as to take effective action on the basis of their understanding....Otherwise there can be no genuine participation, but only the imposition of the ideas of those who are linguistically capable (para 2.2).

As *Kingman* suggests, language is always involved in interactions with communication technologies. The *Cox Report* (1989), which followed *Kingman*, devoted a chapter to 'Media Rducation and Information Technology' within English, recognising the special position of English as a context for developing knowledge, skills and understanding. *Cox* also emphasised how children's awareness of language and meanings, both critical and practical, is involved:

> Media education and information technology alike enlarge pupils' critical understanding of how messages are generated, conveyed and interpreted in different media. First-hand use of media equipment (eg in making videos) and other technologies (such as desk-top publishing) can contribute to children's practical understanding of how meanings are created (para 8.2).

The 1989 NC for English therefore included 'those aspects of media education and information technology which contribute most directly to the central aim of English: to widen the range of children's understanding and use of language, and to develop their skills in it' (*Cox* 9.4).

Assessment, it was pointed out, should be concerned with this understanding and these skills, rather than with knowledge about and confidence in using IT and media technologies as such.

In the 1995 NC, Information Technology is a subject with programmes of study and level descriptions in its own right. It is also, in common with 'Use of language', mentioned as a cross-curricular 'common requirement' in the preface to all the other subjects of the NC. For example:

> Pupils should be given opportunities, where appropriate, to develop and apply their information technology (IT) capability in their study of English (p.1).

We have already seen in Chapters 2 and 3 how the programmes of study for English specifically refer to 'IT-based reference materials' at both KS1 and KS2 (pp.6 and 13) in respect of children's range of reading and the key skills involved. Similarly, in respect of writing skills it is specifically stated that children should plan, draft and improve their work 'on paper and on screen', again both at KS1 and 2 (p9 and p15).

It is a surprising feature of the 1995 NC that the opportunities for children to encounter texts from different media in contexts other than that of information retrieval in AT2, are not explicitly referred to until the KS3 and 4 programmes of study for Reading:

> Pupils should be introduced to a wide range of media, *eg magazines, newspapers, radio, television, film.* They should be given opportunities to analyse and evaluate such material, which should be of high quality and represent a range of forms and purposes, and different structural and presentational devices (DFE, 1995b p20).

It seems surprising that as readers and writers, children will be encountering texts on screen as well as in print for various purposes as language users, but should not have opportunities to reflect critically on media texts in the primary years. In practice such a separation seems unworkable as well as undesirable.

In fact, where Media Education *is* explicitly referred to in the 1995 NC, is in the programmes of study for Speaking and Listening, at least at KS2. As well as giving presentations to audiences 'live or on tape', it is required that pupils 'should be taught to identify and comment on key features of what they see and hear in a variety of media' (p.11) as part of the range of opportunities for oracy. Such opportunities, of course, presuppose viewing or listening to media texts in an informed and critical way.

Information Technology

In the foregoing chapters references to the use of IT have occurred as part of descriptions of classroom practice in English. This is as it should be. The NC requires, as with Standard English and Language Study, that IT (and Media Education) should be thoroughly integrated into the interrelated programmes of speaking and listening, reading and writing activities which make up English. Again this aspect of English is dealt with separately here in recognition of its status as one requiring particular attention in the development of the primary curriculum, and one which also often causes anxiety and confusion.

It is not suggested that IT should be taught separately as a course of decontextualised technical skills. There will often be two facets to activities involving IT : 'learning to use computers and using computers to learn' (Moore and Tweddle, 1992). Although both are necessary, if there is continuity and progression in IT provision the use of computers as a learning tool should ultimately predominate. In what follows, the learning focus is clearly on English in the primary classroom. The situation envisaged is the most common one found there, where one computer (usually an Acorn BBC, Acorn Archimedes or Research Machines model) and one printer, are available to a class on a permanent basis.

IT has a number of different applications with respect to English:

    i)   word processing and desk-top publishing

    ii) concept keyboards

    iii) language development programs

    iv) adventure games and simulations

    v)   information storage and retrieval

    vi) electronic mail

Word processing and desk-top publishing

Word processing software offers the opportunity not only to create printed text, as with an electronic or mechanical typewriter, but most importantly to manipulate that text on screen before it is printed. Desk-top publishing packages are more powerful and offer greater possibilities for manipulation, including the use of graphics and images alongside the written word, as well as more professional-looking hard copy.

For children throughout the primary age-range, the possibility of being able on occasions, to overcome constraints involved in the mechanics of handwriting, and possibly spelling, is a powerful motivating force. Whether teachers type out the text from the drafts of young or struggling writers, or children use their own keyboard skills, the resulting product enhances children's views of themselves as writers and of the power of the written word. For many children this is the spur to further composition.

However, even more important than this, is the facility which IT offers for manipulating words and pictures on the screen, for enabling children to engage with the *process* of writing. Uniquely, the computer allows children to see their writing as a whole, to be able to alter it editorially by inserting, deleting and moving text, as well as to proof-read, correct and save it before publication. The processes of drafting and revision, frequently confused with fair copying in handwritten versions, become viable procedures for all children on screen, given sufficient time and access to the computer. The nature of the computer screen also makes more possible collaborative creation and revision of text, since a pair or small group can easily see the words together and see the effect of possible alterations instantly.

Word processing software for the primary school includes the following (publishers' addresses in the Appendix):

- WRITE (RM 480z and Nimbus), Flexible Software Ltd.
- ALLWRITE (RM Nimbus) ILECC
- VIEW (BBC Master), Acornsoft
- FOLIO (BBC, Archimedes), ESM
- PENDOWN and PENDOWN PLUS (BBC, Archimedes, 480z), Longman-Logotron

In addition to the writing activities suggested above, programs such as ALLWRITE or FOLIO also allow writing and printing in different languages, such as Panjabi, Bengali and Gujarati. Multilingual word processors such as these, open up IT for bilingual children as well as providing opportunities for all pupils to increase their awareness of other languages and scripts. Writing, names, or notices, can easily be transcribed into different community languages, dual-text books produced and a genuine multilingual environment created.

Desk-top publishing software for the primary school would include:

- IMPRESSION JUNIOR (Archimedes), Computer Concepts
- NEWSPA (RM Nimbus), SPA

Activities which exploit the potential of these programs would include the following:

- producing authentic texts for real audiences in the community (letters, questionnaires, guide books, newsletters etc)
- producing a class or school magazine, poetry anthology, illustrated story collection etc.
- presenting children's work for display in the classroom, school or other public areas

Software which allows children to work within specific media forms, such as the newspaper or teletext screen, is also available. Some programs enable writing to be published in columns, with space for headlines, adverts, pictures and so on, to give the appearance of newspaper layout both on the screen and when printed. Others allow teletext pages to be assembled on screen in a variety of colours and with scrolling message banners. These programs have greater limitations and less flexibility than IMPRESSION or NEWSPA, but can form a useful bridge between word processing and genuine desk-top publication. Examples are (newspapers unless stated):

- FRONT PAGE EXTRA and SPECIAL EDITION (BBC), MEP, Newman Software
- FLEET STREET EDITOR (BBC), Mirrorsoft Ltd
- NEWSMASTER (Archimedes, RM Nimbus), LTS

- NEWSMASTER 2 (Archimedes, RM Nimbus), Cambridge-shire Software House
- NEWS BULLETIN (BBC), Newman Software [teletext]

Another group of programs which stops short of full desk-top facilities allows KS1 children to combine text and pictures to create stories which can be published for a variety of audiences and purposes:

- FAIRY TALES (BBC), Resource. Pictures from a disc library can be combined with text to form pages of a book. Demonstration stories can be read on screen.
- DESK TOP STORIES (Archimedes), Resource. An enhanced version of the above, allowing creation of stories using more advanced graphics.

As well as giving infant children access to an appropriate level of desk-top publishing these programs can also be used with older writers who are making picture books or poetry collections for younger readers.

Concept Keyboards

These alternative keyboards, made up of touch-sensitive squares, are used to replace the normal QWERTY one. Used with a variety of overlays, commercially available or created by the teacher, they increase the flexibility of programs and make them accessible to very young children and to children with a variety of special needs. The overlays allow children to press squares on the keyboard so that text, for example, appears on the screen. Software designed specifically to be used with these keyboards includes:

- CONCEPT (BBC), MESU. Allows teachers to create, edit and use overlay files with many BBC programs
- CAPTION (BBC), MESU. Enables children to add text to screens with pictures and borders, which can be printed as pages
- PROMPT WRITER (BBC), MESU. Simplified word processing program, which can be used with a speech synthesiser.

- TOUCH EXPLORER (BBC), MESU. A 'content-free' framework program which allows pictures, diagrams or maps to be used for the overlay. When appropriate parts of the overlay are touched-text appears on the screen relevant to that area. Note-making, cloze procedure and other activities can be added

Although originally designed for children with special needs, this software has many applications with children of different ages and abilities, particularly TOUCH EXPLORER PLUS. Activities arising out of the use of concept keyboards might be:

- creating simple texts with words and images for display or as book jackets, CD covers, adverts etc
- finding information on a topic for non-fiction writing or reading
- group discussion and decision-making related to the topic being explored
- drama arising out of simple texts created or topic areas of information explored

Language Development Programs

Software available here is diverse and designed to develop language skills varying from structuring narrative and poetry to grammar, punctuation, spelling and reading exercises. The danger with this type of program is that some of them may lend themselves to being used purely as skills practice with no meaningful context in classroom English work: a kind of electronic text book with an infinite stock of language exercises. However, many of them also possess the facility for being adapted for use in particular classrooms and contexts and this should be exploited.

Examples of programs which go beyond simple skills practice are:

- TRAY and CREATE (BBC), MEP
- DISCOVER (Archimedes), LTS
- DEVELOPING TRAY (RM 480z and Nimbus), ILECC. This and the above allow teachers and children to complete and also create text with various levels of deletion. An infant

version is also available. A points scoring system introduces a game element

- WORDPLAY (BBC), MEP. Words are chosen randomly from lists and arranged in phrases according to grammatical patterns (eg adjective, noun, verb, adverb). Children can play with existing words and patterns or create their own

- STORYLINE (BBC), MEP. Ideas are generated randomly which can be developed in storytelling, writing or drama activities (a kind of electronic story dice). Children can add in their own phrases or ideas.

- TRACKS (BBC), MEP. This 'branching' program allows children to construct stories with multiple options. It facilitates the writing of Choose Your Own Adventure books as described in Chapter Three

- BEST 4 LANGUAGE (BBC, Archimedes), ASK. A package of programs for very young children, which includes Words, Words, Words (matching objects with words); Hide and Seek (a memory game); Podd (vocabulary extension, linked to activity books also featuring this character)

Activities which can be integrated with the use of the above are:

- creating stories, poems and adventure books
- developing drama from storylines and branching stories
- discussion related to completing or creating texts with deletion
- games which explore parts of speech and sentence grammar
- word games

Adventure Games and Simulations

These two types of program are closely related. Fantasy adventure games allow children (and teachers!) to make decisions and undertake challenges within an imagined world with its own rules and conventions which they can enter at any time. Simulation programs usually take place in 'real time' and involve immersion in authentic situations and events, using procedures normally followed in those contexts. It is perfectly possible to engage in both kinds of activity without computers of course. However the use of IT increases the potential for involvement and for authenticity.

Examples of popular adventure games in the primary classroom are:

- THE LOST FROG (BBC), ESM. A simple adventure for younger children which involves exploring a garden and house, finding and using things in the process, until they discover the frog. Extensions, allowing children's own adventures to be made, are available

- MALLORY (BBC), MEP. A Cluedo-type adventure where children must find a thief who has stolen a valuable item from Mallory Manor. A different scenario can be created, with other settings, characters and stolen goods

- GRANNY'S GARDEN (BBC), 4Mation Educational Resources. Children must search for the King and Queen hidden by a witch in the Kingdom of the Mountains

- DINOSAUR DISCOVERY (BBC), 4Mation Educational Resources. A precursor to *Jurassic Park*! Children have to piece together how to find and hatch a dinosaur from an egg by following the clues left in the diary of a dead professor

- FLOWERS OF CRYSTAL (BBC), 4Mation Educational Resources. The 'mission' here is to find the last flower of the planet Crystal, ruined by greedy developers. First of all a pot, soil, fertiliser and water have to be found before the quest can begin. Spells need to be used to overcome various obstacles in the way

Fantasy games of this sort can stimulate related language activities of many different kinds. For instance, they can be used as the basis for:

- story writing related to the characters, situations and themes

- creating children's own adventure games

- role play, improvisation and other exploratory drama activities arising from the adventures and developing aspects of them

- collaborative group discussion and problem-solving

Simulation programs are slightly less flexible in operation and usually involve more ancillary materials and other programs (eg word processing). Examples of these and the activities they are intended to give rise to are:

- POLICE — LANGUAGE IN EVIDENCE (BBC, RM Nimbus), Cambridgeshire Software House. The control room of a police station is re-created and appropriate police procedures have to be followed, using spoken and written language, to deal with various incidents (eg taking witness statements, keeping a station log book etc). A visit by local community officers can be combined with the simulation, with children sworn in as special constables for the project, with the possibility of promotion if successful!

- EXTRA (BBC), Shropshire LEA. Here a busy newsroom is simulated. News from a major incident (eg bomb blast in Hyde Park), and less serious ones, comes into the newsroom in real time via a printer operating as a 'teleprinter' machine. The story unfolds rapidly and realistically and children have to react to the news by publishing and broadcasting reports of it through various media. For example, groups can use FRONT PAGE EXTRA to create newspaper articles or NEWS BULLETIN to compile teletext pages. Alternatively they might use audio or video tape to record radio or television news items of specified duration and to a deadline

IT-based simulations can also be created using electronic communication between children in different schools or between a school and students in a university department, for example (see Moore and Tweddle pp45-49 for a case study). This kind of 'live adventuring' becomes increasingly possible with the spread of electronic mail networks to primary schools

Information Storage and Retrieval

Databases can be built up by children from fieldwork surveys or library-based investigations. The following programs allow children to store and retrieve information and to present it in appropriate charts and graphs:

- QUEST (RM 480z and Nimbus, BBC), The Advisory Unit
- GRASS (BBC), Newman Software

This software can provide contexts for the development of study skills involved in ordering, collating and summarising data and in extracting information from it. They might be used, for instance, in the creation of non-fiction books containing tables and charts. However the programs can also be used as part of activities related to fiction texts, enabling readers to compile profiles of characters in novels and plays, for example.

Increasingly, primary schools are also able to access other more powerful databases. The advent of the CD-ROM means that vastly more information can be stored than on the normal floppy disk. Multimedia programs enable video sequences and sound to be included with the text and graphics on the computer screen. Simple multimedia authoring programs such as GENESIS (Oak Solutions), for the Archimedes, also allow children to produce interactive presentations involving text, picture, sound and even video clips, though some additional equipment may be required. Developments such as these bring IT and Media Education ever closer together. As well as having access to encyclopaedic and multimedia stores of information via CD-ROM, primary schools are also able to tap into networks of on-line databases via telephone modems linked to their computers. Both children and teachers are then able to gain access to virtually limitless sources of data.

Electronic Mail

E-mail, or communication between subscribers using computers and a telephone modem, extends the horizon in a similar way in terms of providing audiences and purposes for English activities. Belonging to a national or global network of computer users offers obvious opportunities for links with other schools and communities. Experience suggests that these links need to go beyond simple pen-pal correspondence if they are to be sustained and developed effectively. Authentic contexts need to be created for sending information between schools, such as:

- collecting information (eg on language use or reading/view-ing habits) from other children

- collaborating with other children in the creation and development of a drama or simulation
- collaborating with other children in the writing of stories

Links can also be established with other adults (eg a writer, the warden of a field study centre, an advisory teacher). To succeed, the electronic communication will need to be carefully scheduled and organised and access made possible for all children, not only the more able.

Using IT in the Classroom

In the area of computing, teachers are probably more willing than elsewhere to acknowledge children's existing skills and understanding and allow them to demonstrate their expertise. It is important that experiences outside of school, be they computer games or educational software, should be valued. Children from widely different backgrounds now have access to personal computers and bring to school from an early age skills in these new areas of literacy. These need to be built on in the classroom and unnecessary mystification of computers avoided.

The use of IT in recognisably English contexts is also valuable in challenging stereotyped associations of computers with subjects such as Maths and Science. Alongside such associations often go assumptions that computers particularly appeal to boys or that boys are particularly adept at using them. In English, where boys often underachieve in a mirror image of the position of girls in Maths and Science, the tendency to use IT (and Media Education equipment) to engage boys' interest must be balanced against the necessity of ensuring equal access for girls and boys.

Information Technology, by its very nature, changes rapidly. Software mentioned in this chapter as illustrative examples of IT applications in English will inevitably become dated and superseded by new ones. In the area of fantasy games, for instance, the availability of vastly improved still images, graphics and now video sequences (not to mention 'virtual reality' technology) means that some of the earlier programs with limited or no graphics look very dated already. However, although software and hardware will change quickly, the principles underlying IT usage, the applications suggested for it in the English curriculum and the opportunities mentioned which it can provide, will remain relevant.

Media Education

Similar reflections come to mind concerning Media Education. Here is another rapidly changing field which forms a significant part of children's experience out of school. Children's very earliest encounters with stories and rhymes, for example, are likely to include video and audio tape versions. Increasingly, as they get older, children will meet traditional narratives through the medium of film and television first, often the Walt Disney animated versions of fairy stories. This experience of media productions and growing awareness of the language and conventions of, say, television which goes with it, will need to be the foundation for Media Education in the primary school.

'The media' is a confusing, catch-all term. It can be used to refer to the technology used (print, film, audio tape), the organisations who use them (newspapers, publishers, film studios, radio stations) and also the productions which result (newspapers, cinema films, radio programmes). 'Media Education' also requires careful definition:

> Media education... seeks to increase children's critical understanding of the media — namely, television, film, video, radio, photography, popular music, printed materials and computer software. How they work, how they produce meaning, how they are organised and how audiences make sense of them, are the issues that media education addresses. [It] aims to develop systematically children's critical and creative powers through analysis and production of media artefacts. (Bazalgette ed., 1989)

Media education is not only concerned then, with film and television, but with all forms of public communication, including those using the medium of print and including the computer programs discussed above. As with I.T., Media Education (as distinct from Media Studies in the secondary school) is fundamentally cross-curricular, particularly in its productive aspect. Children can make newspapers, shoot videos, take photographs in History-, Geography- or Science-based activities as often as in English ones, as previous chapters have suggested. It is in its 'critical', even more so than its 'creative' aspect, that Media Education has particular affinities with English (though both aspects should always be present in media work). 'Reading' media 'texts' and 'genres', considering their language, structure and conventions, can be seen as an extension of the kind of critical approach to literary texts and to language study traditionally used in English. As the *Cox Report* (1989) pointed out, Media Education, like the study of literature, always 'deals with fundamental aspects of language, interpretation and meaning.'

As with IT, the NC makes it clear that Media Education should be part of an integrated programme which develops oracy and literacy, and not another subject in an already overcrowded primary curriculum. The *Non-Statutory Guidance* (1990) and Bazalgette (1991) suggest three approaches to media texts and the questions which they generate:

- *Media languages*: What does the text say? How does it say it? What type of text is it?
- *Producers and audiences*: How was the text produced? By whom and for whom? Why?
- *Representation*: Is it supposed to be like real life? Do you find it convincing? What might other people think?

Examples are given in the *Non-Statutory Guidance* of integrated English-based projects which allow exploration of these aspects of media education. (sections D19-20). A KS1 project 'Taking Photographs' is detailed, which involves young children taking still photographs of each other, giving directions for how they want to be represented, keeping records of how the photograph was taken and finally comparing the printed copies with the intentions behind them. Preparation beforehand involved examining photographs from different sources, including ones from home, and discussing how they were made, who took them and where they could be found. Since most of the photos were of the children themselves at different times the project would fit in well both with introductory work on 'Ourselves' and with considering 'Change' as part of the History curriculum.

The example at KS2 is of a project on 'The Local Area', with obvious links to the Geography programmes of study. Here the children began by looking at local publications (newspapers, tourist information, adverts) and discussing their producers and likely audiences, as well as the way they use language and visual images. They then produced displays of the locality using photographs and captions. The aim was to produce different displays for different audiences: tourists, businessmen, children etc. This involved the children working in groups planning, producing and presenting their words and photos using appropriate techniques and conventions. The displays were evaluated in the light of the original intentions and the different representations of the local area compared. Follow-up activities also involved considering the use of locations in fiction and non-fiction both in print and on screen.

Both of these projects provided contexts for speaking and listening, reading and writing activities. The children were able to reflect on and to create media texts, considering at appropriate levels and in meaningful ways, the questions above concerned with media languages, producers, audiences and representation. Both used photography as the central medium to be explored, reflecting a well-established view that the still camera and its products offer an ideal way into Media Education at any level, offering easily available technology and a clear, manageable and relevant focus for attention. Other activities which involve close scrutiny of visual images and photos might include:

- looking at puzzle pictures (optical illusions, spot the differences, etc.)
- comparing paintings and photographs
- experimenting with changing the frames for photographs to include more or less of the image ('cropping')
- adding different captions to photographs
- sequencing a series of photographs or pictures to tell a story (or stories)
- creating photo-stories (often found in children's comics and magazines)

This might, if appropriate, lead on from experience and reflection, as with Language Study, to more formal analysis using the distinctive methodology of Media Studies. This would involve considering the procedures of 'Image Analysis', which deconstructs visual images through careful consideration first of what they *denote*, what is actually visible in them, then of what they *connote*, what the images might stand for or suggest. Commercially available packages from the British Film

Institute (BFI) Education Department, such as *Reading Pictures* and *Picture Stories* (1986), provide material for this type of analysis. Andrew Bethell's *Eyeopeners I* (1982) and *The Visit*, published by the English and Media Centre, can also be used with older primary children.

It certainly isn't necessary to use expensive and sophisticated equipment to provide worthwhile opportunities for Media Education. None of the above activities require more than the kind of materials easily available to most teachers. Other basic school equipment such as the overhead projector and the slide projector can be commandeered to extend work on the still image. Children can use overhead transparencies to draw simple picture sequences (or photocopy images onto them); music or sound effects to accompany the sequence, as it is gradually revealed, can then be recorded onto cassette tape. Alternatively, a conventional tape/slide presentation can be used, though this is less flexible and a little more expensive. The technological challenge of synchronising image and sound in this sort of context gives children an insight into media production, audience and representation at an appropriate level.

However, new technology now available to primary schools makes it possible to extend exploration of the visual image even further. The still video camera, for example, a palm-size camera which records colour pictures on a floppy disk, can be connected to a television to give immediate, full size images on the screen. These can also be copied onto video tape to be saved, or for a sound track to be added later. The increased opportunities for reflection and discussion as well as for production of media texts are obvious.

The wide availability of small, easy-to use camcorders along with the now universal video recorder and player has widened the horizons for Media Education in the primary school. It is now a much more realistic proposition to give young children the chance to criticise and to create moving images. The danger now lies in being over-ambitious. Rather than plunge into viewing or making extended videos, it is much more effective to concentrate on small-scale projects with achievable goals. This might involve children planning, designing and videoing short animated sequences, making their own television adverts or constructing the title sequence for a new programme. The video camera can be a resource for children to use in exploring their own experiences in and out of school, by compiling video diaries, creating a 'video letter' to send to another school, recording interviews with visitors to school or making a record of a school visit.

Adverts and title sequences also provide an appropriate context for *talking about* television. Again, this sort of discussion will be grounded in children's considerable experience outside of school. Initial activities such as viewing sequences without words, or listening to a sound-track with the screen covered, will enable children to begin to appreciate how television and film are deliberately constructed media, rather than the neutral 'windows' they are often passively viewed as.

Media Education can equally well deal with the printed word and the spoken word, with comics, newspapers, magazines, popular music and radio as well as television, video and film. Examples of appropriate activities here might be:

comics:
- cutting up comic strips and reordering them
- comparing good and bad characters or girl and boy characters in different comics;
- combining pages from a range of comics to make one ideal publication

newspapers:
- looking at the language and style of different papers
- comparing coverage of the same news item in several papers
- producing a class newspaper using an appropriate journalistic style as well as appropriate presentation;

radio:
- creating short radio plays with sound effects
- recording a series of 'Desert Island Books' programmes
- making trailers to introduce pop music records, giving background information and critical assessment

advertising:
- looking at the packaging of popular products

- creating names for new products and designing a campaign;
- looking at adverts aimed at children.

As with Information Technology, the aim of all these activities must be to demystify the media, to create informed and critical consumers who can 'identify and comment on key features of what they see and hear in a variety of media', as the 1995 NC for English now legally requires. Extending children's active and reflective reading habits from literary texts to include those produced by different media — not replacing traditional skills but augmenting them — will provide opportunities in English which will prepare children for the literacy demands of the next century.

Further Reading

Information Technology

Minns, H. (1991) *Primary Language — Extending the Curriculum with Computers*. Coventry: NCET.

Moore, P. and Tweddle, S. (1992) *The Integrated Classroom: Language, Learning and IT,* London: Hodder and Stoughton.

NATE (1990) *IT's English: Accessing English with Computers* [2nd ed]. Sheffield: NATE.

NCC (1990) *Non-Statutory Guidance for Information Technology,* London: HMSO.

Media Education

Bazalgette, C. (1991) *Media Education,* London: Hodder and Stoughton.

Craggs, C. (1992) *Media Education in the Primary School,* London: Routledge.

Emerson, A. (1993) *Teaching Media in the Primary School,* London: Cassell.

Harpley, A. (1990) *Bright Ideas; Media Education.* Leamington Spa: Scholastic.

Appendix

Addresses for computer software and Media Education materials

Acornsoft, Acorn Computers Ltd., Fulbourn Road, Cambridge, CB1 4JN.

The Advisory Unit, Endymion Road, Hatfield, Herts. AL10 8AU.

ASK (Applied Systems Knowledge) Ltd., London House, 68 Upper Richmond Road, London SW15 2RP.

BFI (British Film Institute), Education Dept., 21 Stephen Street, London, W1P 1PL.

Cambridgeshire Software House, The Town Hall, St Ives, Huntingdon, Cambs.

Computer Concepts, Gaddeston Place, Hemel Hempstead, Herts. HP2 6EX.

The English and Media Centre, 136 Chalton Street, London, NW1 1RX.

ESM, Duke Street, Wisbech, Cambs. PE13 2AE.

Flexible Software Ltd., PO Box 100, Abingdon, Oxon. OX13 6PQ.

4Mation Educational Resources, Linden Lea, Rock Park, Barnstaple, Devon, EX32 9AQ.

ILECC [now Capital Media], John Ruskin Street, London, SE5 0PQ.

Longman-Logotron, Dales Brewery, Gwydir Street, Cambridge CB1 2LJ.

LTS (Learning and Training Systems Ltd.), Haddon House, Alcester Road, Studley, Warwicks., B80 7AN.

MAPE (Micros and Primary Education), Newman Software, Genners Lane, Bartley Green, Birmingham, B32 3NT.

MEP (Micro Electronics in Education Project): these programs can now be obtained through Local Education Authorities.

MESU (Micro Electronics Support Unit Manchester Polytechnic, Hathersage Road, Manchester, M13 8AJ.

Mirrorsoft Ltd., Maxwell House, 74 Worship Streeet, London, EC2A 2EN.

Oak Solutions, Suite 25, Robin Enterprise Centre, Leeds Road, Idle, West Yorks. BD10 9TE.

Resource, Exeter Road, Wheatley, Doncaster, DN2 4PY.

SPA (Software Production Associates Ltd.), PO Box 59, Leamington Spa, Warwicks., CV31 3QA.

Shropshire LEA, Educational Computing Centre, Racecourse Crescent, Shrewsbury, SY2 5BP.

References

Abrahams, R. (1985) *Afro-American Folktales*. New York: Pantheon .

Adams, M.J. (1990) *Beginning to Read.: Thinking and Learning about Print*. Cambridge, Mass.: MIT.

Ahlberg, J. and Ahlberg, A. (1986) *The Jolly Postman*. London: Heinemann.

Armitage, R. and Armitage, D. (1977) *The Lighthouse Keeper's Lunch*. London: Andre Deutsch.

Arnott, K. (1962) *African Myths and Legends*. Oxford: Oxford University Press.

Ashley, B. (1981) *I'm Trying To Tell You*. Harmonsworth: Kestrel

Assessment of Performance Unit (1981) *Language Performance in Schools: Primary Survey Report No.1*. London: HMSO.

Assessment of Performance Unit (1982) *Language Performance in Schools: Secondary Survey Report No.1*. London: HMSO.

Bain, R. (1991) *Reflections: Talking about Language*. London: Hodder and Stoughton.

Bain, R., Fitzgerald, B. and Taylor, M. (1992) *Looking into Language*. London: Hodder and Stoughton.

Bazalgette, C.(1989) [ed] *Primary Media Education: A Curriculum Statement*. London: BFI.

Bazalgette, C. (1991) *Media Education*. London: Hodder and Stoughton.

Beard, R. (1990) *Developing Reading 3-13* (2nd ed). London: Hodder and Stoughton.

Bentley, D. and Rowe, A. (1991) *Group Reading in the Primary Classroom*. University of Reading: Reading and Language Information Centre.

Benton, M. and Fox, G. (1985) *Teaching Literature 9-14*. Oxford: Oxford University Press.

Bereiter, C. and Scardamalia, M. (1987) *The Psychology of Written Composition*. New Jersey: Lawrence Erlbaum.

Bethell, A. (1982) *Eyeopeners 1*. Cambridge: Cambridge University Press.

Britton, J. et al. (1975) *The Development of Writing Abilities (11-18)*. Basingstoke: Macmillan.

Brown, J. (1968) *Flat Stanley*. London; Methuen.

Brownjohn, S. (1994) *To Rhyme Or Not To Rhyme?* London: Hodder and Stoughton.

Brownjohn,S. and Whitaker, J. (1995) *Word Games*. London: Hodder and Stoughton.

Bryant, P. and Bradley, L. (1985) *Children's Reading Problems*. Oxford: Blackwell.

Bryant, P. (1994) 'Reading Research Update', *Child Education*, 71,10.

Bullock Report (1975) *A Language For Life*. London: HMSO.

Burnett, F.H. (1911) *The Secret Garden*. London: Heinemann.

Byars,B. (1976) *The TV Kid*. London: The Bodley Head.

Cairney, T. (1990) *Teaching Reading Comprehension*. Buckingham: Open University Press.

Carter, R. (1990) [ed] *Knowledge About Language and the Curriculum: the LINC Reader*. London: Hodder and Stoughton.

Christie, F. (1989) *Writing in Schools*. Geelong: Deakin University Press.

Crosher, J. (1989) *Schools*. London: Hodder and Stoughton.

Clegg, A. (1969) [ed] *The Excitement of Writing*. London: Chatto and Windus.

Corbett, P. and Moses, B. (1986) *Catapults and Kingfishers*. Oxford: Oxford University Press.

Cox, B. and Dyson, A.. (1969) [eds] *Fight For Education*. London: Critical Quarterly Society.

Cox Report (1989) *English for ages 5-16*. London: HMSO.

Cox, B. (1991) *Cox on Cox*. London: Hodder and Stoughton.

Crystal, D. (1994) 'Which English — or English *Which* ? 'in Hayhoe, M. and Parker, S. [eds] *Who Owns English?* Buckingham: Open University Press.

Dahl, R. (1970) *Fantastic Mr Fox*.London: George Allen and Unwin.

Dahl, R. (1982) *The BFG*. London: Jonathan Cape.

Davies, G. (1988) 'Taking children's writing seriously', in Styles, M. and Triggs, P., *Poetry 0-16*. London: Books for Keeps.

Davies, Y. (1986) *Picture Stories*. London: British Film Institute.

DES (1989) *English in the National Curriculum*. London:HMSO.

DES (1992) *Curriculum Organisation and Classroom Practice in Primary Schools*. London: HMSO.

DFE (1993a) *English for ages 5-16 (1993)*. London: HMSO.

DFE (1993b) *The Initial Training of Primary School Teachers*. London: HMSO.

DFE (1995a) *Key Stages 1 and 2 of the National Curriculum*. London: HMSO.

DFE (1995b) *English in the National Curriculum*. London: HMSO.

Dixon, J. (1967) *Growth Through English*. Reading: NATE.

Doonan, J. (1993) *Looking at Pictures in Picture Books*. Stroud: Thimble Press.

Doughty, P. et al (1971) *Language in Use*. London: Edward Arnold.

Ferreiro, E. and Teberosky, A. (1983) *Literacy Before Schooling*. Exeter, New Hampshire: Heinemann.

Garfield, L. (1993) *Romeo and Juliet* [abridgement]. London: Heinemann.

Gentry, R. (1987) *Spel...is a Four-Letter Word*. Leamington Spa: Scholastic.

Gilbert, P. (1990) 'Authorizing disadvantage', in Christie, F. [ed] *Literacy for a Changing World*. Hawthorn, Victoria: ACER.

Goodman, K.(1973) 'Miscues: Windows on the Reading Process', in Goodman, K. [ed] *Miscue Analysis, Applications to Reading Instruction*. Urbana, Illinois: ERIC.

Gorman, T., Hutchison, D. and Trimble, J. (n.d.) *Reading in Reform: The Avon Collaborative Reading Project*. Windsor: NFER.

Graves, D. (1983) *Writing: Teachers and Children at Work*. Oxford: Heinemann.

Gregory, A., Keiner, J., Lyons, H. and Redfern, A. (1990) *Writers' Workshops: On Becoming a Writer*. Stoke-on-Trent: Trentham.

Hall, N. (1987) *The Emergence of Literacy*. London: Hodder and Stoughton.

Harris, J. and Wilkinson, J. (1990) [eds] *A Guide to English Language in the National Curriculum*. Cheltenham: Stanley Thornes.

Hawkins, E. (1987) *Awareness of Language: An Introduction*. Cambridge: Cambridge University Press.

Haynes, J. (1992) *A Sense of Words*. London: Hodder and Stoughton.

HMI (1984) *English from 5 to 16: Curriculum Matters 1*. London: HMSO.

HMI (1986) *Responses to Curriculum Matters 1*. London: HMSO.

HMI (1990) *The Teaching and Learning of Reading in Primary Schools*. London: HMSO.

Hudson, R. (1992) *Teaching Grammar*. Oxford: Blackwell.

Hughes, T. (1968) *The Iron Man*. London: Faber.

Hunt, G. (1994) *Inspirations for Grammar*. Leamington Spa: Scholastic.

ILEA (1988) *The Primary Language Record: Handbook for Teachers*. London: CLPE.

Isherwood, S. (1988) *William's Problems*. London: Macdonald.

Jarman, C. (1979) *The Development of Handwriting Skills*. Oxford: Blackwell.

Kemp, G. (1985) *Jason Bodger and the Priory Ghost*. London: Faber.

Kingman Report (1988) *Report of the Committee of Inquiry into the Teaching of English Language*. London: HMSO.

King-Smith, D. (1988) *George Speaks*. Harmondsworth: Viking/Kestrel.

Kitamura, S. and Oram, H. (1982) *Angry Arthur*. London: Andersen Press.

Kroll, B. (1981) 'Developmental relationships between speaking and writing', in Kroll, B. and Vann, R. [eds] *Exploring Speaking-Writing Relationships*. Urbana, Illinois: NCTE.

Lewis, M. and Wray, D. (1994) *Working Paper 6: Extending interactions with non-fiction texts*. University of Exeter: EXEL Project.

Lewis, M. and Wray, D.(n.d.) *Writing Frames*. University of Exeter: EXEL Project.

Lewis, M. and Wray, D. (1995) *Developing Children's Non-Fiction Writing: Working with Writing Frames*. Leamington Spa: Scholastic

Littlefair, A. (1990) *Reading All Types of Writing*. Buckingham: Open University Press.

Lockwood, M. (1993) 'Getting into the rhythm: children reading poetry'. *Reading*, 27, 3.

Lunzer, E. and Gardner, K. (1979) *The Effective Use of Reading*. London: Heinemann.

Lunzer, E. and Gardner, K. (1984) *Learning from the Written Word*. Edinburgh: Oliver and Boyd.

Mackay, D., Thompson, B., and Schaub, P. (1979) *Breakthrough to Literacy: Teacher's Manual* [2nd ed]. London: Longman.

Mark, J. (1976) *Thunder and Lightnings*. Harmondsworth: Kestrel.

Mark, J. (1977) *Under the Autumn Garden*. Harmondsworth: Kestrel.

Mark, J. (1982) *The Dead Letter Box*. London: Hamish Hamilton.

McKee, D. (1980) *Not Now, Bernard*. London: Andersen Press.

Meek, M. (1988) *How Texts Teach What Readers Learn*. Stroud: Thimble Press.

Moon, C. (n.d.) *Assessing Reading Strategies at Key Stage 1*. University of Reading: Reading and Language Information Centre.

Moon, C. and Raban, B.(1992) *A Question of Reading*. London: David Fulton.

Moon, C. (1994) 'The literacy environment', in Webster A.and Webster [eds] *Supporting Learning in the Primary School*. Bristol: Avec Designs.

Moon, C. (1995) *Individualised Reading* [26th ed]. University of Reading: Reading and Language Information Centre.

Moore, P. and Tweddle, S. (1992) *The Integrated Classroom: Language, Learning and IT*. London: Hodder and Stoughton.

NATE (1990) *IT's English: Accessing English with Computers* [2nd ed]. Sheffield: NATE.

NCC (1989) *English Key Stage 1: Non-Statutory Guidance*. York: NCC.

NCC (1990) *English Non-Statutory Guidance*. York: NCC.

NCC (1992) *National Curriculum English: The Case For Revising the Order*. York: NCC.

NCC (1993a) *Evaluation of the Implementation of English in the National Curriculum at Key Stages 1,2 and 3 (1991-93). Final Report*. York: NCC.

NCC (1993b) *NCC Consultation Report: English*. York: NCC.

Neate, B. (1992) *Finding Out About Finding Out*. London: Hodder and Stoughton.

Newbolt Report (1921) *The Teaching of English in England*. London: HMSO.

Newman, J. (1984) *The Craft of Children's Writing*. Ontario: Scholastic.

NOP (1991) *Teaching Talking and Learning in KS2*. York: NCC.

Norman, K. (1990) *Teaching Talking and Learning in KS1*. York: NCC.

NWP (1987) *Drawing on Experience: A Picture Planning Approach to Writing*. [draft materials, SCDC]

NWP (1989) *Responding to Children's Writing*. Walton-on-Thames: Nelson.

NWP (1989) *Writing and Learning*. Walton-on-Thames: Nelson.

Perera, K. (1984) *Children's Writing and Reading*. Oxford: Blackwell.

Pinkwater, D. (1992) *I Was a Class 2 Werewolf.* Basingstoke: Macmillan.

Redfern, A. (1993) *Spelling and Language Skills.* Leamington Spa: Scholastic.

Rosen, M. and McGough, R. (1979) *You Tell Me.* Harmondsworth: Kestrel.

Rosen, M. (1989) *Did I Hear You Write?* London: Andre Deutsch.

Sassoon, R. (1983) *The Practical Guide to Children's Handwriting.* London: Thames and Hudson.

SCAA (1994a) *English in the National Curriculum: Draft Proposals.* London: HMSO.

SCAA (1994b) *The National Curriculum Orders: English* [page proofs]. London: HMSO.

SEAC (1991a) *School Assessment Folder KS1.* London: HMSO.

SEAC (1991b) *Children's Work Assessed: English, KS1.* London: HMSO.

SEAC (1991c) *Handbook of Guidance for the SAT.* London: HMSO.

SEAC (1993) *Assessment Handbook: English.* London: HMSO.

Sendak, M. (1967) *Where the Wild Things Are.* London: Bodley Head.

Smith, F. (1982) *Writing and the Writer.* London: Heinemann.

Smith, F. (1985) *Reading* [2nd ed]. Cambridge: Cambridge University Press.

Southgate, V. Arnold, H. and Johnson, S. (1981) *Extending Beginning Reading.* London: Heinemann.

Tann, S. (1991) *Developing Language in the Primary Classroom.* London: Cassell.

Tomlinson, J. (1968) *The Owl Who Was Afraid of the Dark.* London: Methuen.

Torbe, M. (1978) *Teaching Spelling* [2nd ed]. London: Ward Lock.

Trudgill, P. (1975) *Accent, Dialect and the School.* London: Edward Arnold.

Ure, J. (1987) *A Tea-Leaf on the Roof.* London: Blackie.

Wray, D. and Medwell, J. (1991) *Literacy and Language in the Primary Years.* London: Routledge.

Wells, G. (1987)*The Meaning Makers.* London: Hodder and Stoughton.

Willis, J. and Ross, T. (1990) *Dr Xargle's Book of Earth Tiggers.* London: Andersen Press.

INDEX